U.S. International
Trade Regulation

U.S. International Trade Regulation

A Primer

William H. Lash III

The AEI Press

Publisher for the American Enterprise Institute
WASHINGTON, D.C.

1998

Available in the United States from the AEI Press, c/o Publisher Resources Inc., 1224 Heil Quaker Blvd., P.O. Box 7001, La Vergne, TN 37086-7001; call toll free 1-800-269-6267. Distributed outside the United States by arrangement with Eurospan, 3 Henrietta Street, London WC2E 8LU England.

Library of Congress Cataloging-in-Publication Data
Lash, William H., III
  U.S. international trade regulation : a primer / William H. Lash III.
    p. cm.
  Includes bibliographical references and index.
  ISBN 0-8447-3930-8 (cloth : alk. paper). — ISBN 0-8447-3931-6 (pbk. : alk. paper).
  1. Foreign trade regulation—United States. 2. International business enterprises—Law and legislation—United States.
  I. Title.
  KF1976.L275   1998
  343.73'087—dc21   98-45089
                                                         CIP

1 3 5 7 9 10 8 6 4 2

THE AEI PRESS
Publisher for the American Enterprise Institute
1150 17th Street, N.W., Washington, D.C. 20036

Printed in the United States of America

To my bride, Sharon, and Will

Contents

Acknowledgment

Special thanks to Robert B. Parker for his invaluable thoughts and contributions to this project. I would also like to thank Jeffrey Atik, James Burnham, David Henderson, George Kleinfeld, and Murray Weidenbaum for their valuable comments and advice. Research assistance from Gerald Koenig, J. Linwood Smith, and Deborah Wengel is greatly appreciated.

U.S. International Trade Regulation

1
Introduction

International trade has always played an important role in American political life. At times, trade issues have been woven into a larger pattern of events that shaped a broader political debate. At other times, notably in the late nineteenth century and perhaps again at the end of the twentieth, international trade has emerged as an important and defining political issue in its own right.

The debate today pits free traders against those who are not. The latter typically proclaim themselves fair traders, although their critics often label them protectionists—an epithet that, since the days of the Smoot-Hawley Tariff Act, has been an insult akin to disparagement of one's intelligence or lineage. Indeed, a strong constituency is apparently forming across the political spectrum against a policy of free trade, at least as an abstract notion.

As in most political debate, the labels tend to hide more than they reveal. Ronald Reagan was the most ardent of recent presidents in his support for free and open markets, but he intervened in the international trade of goods more than any of his predecessors. His successor, George Bush, was noted not for his strong laissez-faire credentials, but as a strong advocate and practitioner of open trade. The Reagan administration tended to view international trade issues as an extension of domestic politics, while the Bush administration viewed international trade as part of its foreign policy agenda.

Indeed, U.S. trade policy in many ways reflects the result of the continuing tension between these two views. With the possible exception of the war powers, no other area of U.S. policy has generated the level of interbranch rivalry as international trade. Under the Constitution, Congress has the plenary authority to regulate foreign commerce, but the president presides over foreign policy and the formulation of international agreements. More often than not, and particularly in recent decades, presidents have tended to view international trade as a foreign policy tool. Congress as a whole has taken a view that links international trade more closely to domestic interests. The agencies that regulate trade in this country, the laws that they implement, and the nature of the international legal system—all reflect to a greater or lesser extent this unique tension in the structure of American government.

Much of the political drama during Bill Clinton's first two years as president was provided by two international trade agreements, the North American Free Trade Agreement (NAFTA) and the General Agreement on Tariffs and Trade (GATT). The political economy of these agreements was unusual and reflected the political shift underway across political lines. Domestic business interests were divided. Organized labor was opposed, although the agreements presented an opportunity for increased employment in mostly nonunionized sectors of the economy. The Democratic president prevailed, but with the support of congressional Republicans—and over the active opposition of the congressional leadership of the president's own party. Much of the foregoing is evident from a close reading of the daily press. But the popular political debate obscures the concerns at the heart of trade relations today. The GATT and NAFTA, the various agreements of industrial countries under the auspices of the Organization for Economic Cooperation and Development, bilateral investment and commercial arrangements, and many national laws and regulations defy such all-encompassing notions as free or protectionist. The most ardent free traders in the field have been the most ardent supporters of the most draconian trade remedies. Similarly, economists who favor open trade usually lament the indiscriminate use of trade remedies or the application of trade remedies by government agencies but not all trade remedies themselves.

The complex regulations that govern international trade today form an arcane and often opaque legal regime. The Internal Revenue Code has been favorably compared with the U.S. laws on international trade in terms of clarity and precision. In addition, the Internal Revenue Code applies universally. Many consumers are "taxed" by the application of the international trade laws without realizing it or appreciating the goals that the trade laws seek to serve. This is the point addressed by this volume.

I start with a broad proposition: the days in which the trade question amounted to higher or lower import barriers, mostly tariffs, are bygone. Although "spikes" in the tariff schedules—high tariffs on specific items—still exist in the United States and other countries, most of the world's trade, trade among industrial nations, is conducted on a duty-free or low-tariff basis. Protecting the industrial interests of a country such as the United States simply by imposing new tariff measures or other barriers to imports would require a complete overhaul of domestic law and international institutions.

A brief list of the key issues that generated the most controversy during the debate over the most recent GATT agreement illustrates this point: Should agriculture and textiles be subject to the international trade regime, or should they continue to be treated as special cases? Should antidumping procedures be more rigorous? How should pure research and development subsidies be treated in countervailing duty determinations? To what extent should trade in services be subject to international discipline, and what services (telecommunications, finance, professional services) should be included?

There was a move by the Uruguay Round of the GATT to lower many existing tariffs; this was not particularly controversial and was often advocated by the industries that the tariffs were initially intended to protect. How did this come about? The answer is simple: this is what the United States government wanted. Beginning with the Wilson administration in 1916, the United States has taken an increasingly legalistic view of international trade issues. The focus has shifted from protecting particular industries to imposing targeted sanctions on trade activity deemed unfair. Administrative procedures have therefore come to replace protection per se as the driving force in the regulation of domestic trade. Following World War II, the United States was in a position to guide the development of a new international trade regime and did so with the establishment of an international trade code (the GATT).

But the changing nature of the international economy, particularly the industrial economies of North America, Western Europe, and Japan, is an important factor. The issue has several components. Initially, what is the official attitude toward those changes? Are we as a nation committed to retaining the industries that employed preceding generations, for example, automobile, steel, textiles, and at what cost? If the cost is the competitiveness of nascent industries such as biotechnology and advanced communications, are we still willing to do so? To what extent are we willing to cede the older industries to newly industrializing nations, on the theory that they will be the customers of our twenty-first-century industries? These questions have economic and social implications of profound import; the NAFTA and GATT agreements reflected a decision, sometimes only implicitly revealed in popular debate, to move in favor of emerging industries and newly industrialized markets.

The recent revolution in manufacturing and transport technologies has also colored international trade issues. Traditionally, countries rich in raw materials traded for manufactured goods—in David Ricardo's original defense of free trade, Portugal traded port wine for English cloth. Today, with improvements in transportation, a larger volume of international trade is in the form of component parts. An automobile might have an American chassis, a motor assembled in Mexico, and Japanese electronics; final assembly might occur in Canada. By some estimates, one-quarter to one-third of all U.S. imports and exports are intracorporate transfers between affiliated companies. Manufacturing on a global scale would have been considered madness only a generation or two ago because of problems of communication and coordination. The joint manufacturing effort succeeds now because the design and production efforts, though continents apart, are well integrated.

Regulating trade in these circumstances changes the nature of the debate. A traditional precept of trade regulation held that import restrictions provided material benefit to concentrated domestic industries, with small and diffuse effects on a broad number of consumers. When the trade restriction is imposed on a component part, however, the consumer is itself an industry that employs workers and capital and generates domestic economic activity. If it faces substantial international competition from firms that do not face restrictions on access to their component parts, the consumer industry cannot pass along its increased costs without placing itself at a competitive disadvantage. A recent case in international trade concerning large mechanical transfer presses imported from Japan illustrates the point. These presses are the huge, sophisticated machines that auto manufacturers use to stamp steel plate into panels for auto bodies. Sophisticated transfer presses allow auto manufacturers to change model designs in little time and with great precision—an ability that U.S. auto companies need to remain competitive.

Whether or not trade officials provide relief in these circumstances, they have implicitly made a choice regarding the relative merits of two industries. On what basis should that choice be made: an economic analysis of each industry's relative contribution to the gross domestic product, the impact on consumer welfare, employment in each industry, the contribution to the country's technology base? Because this case was brought under the dumping laws, none of these questions was raised; rather, the terms of the law were manipulated to reach the specified result.

Had the matter been raised under another provision of the trade laws, such as section 201 (chapter 5), these questions could have been highly material to the domestic industry's chances of success and, in that event, to the nature of the trade remedy offered. The most famous case under that statute concerned Harley-Davidson, the domestic motorcycle manufacturer. Harley successfully pursued a section 201 action and was granted limited relief. The company achieved a public relations coup when it asked the government to remove the remedy before the scheduled date. But that happy outcome depended on a series of factors that even well-intentioned and omniscient regulators could not possibly replicate in other cases. Section 201 has not achieved nearly that level of success for other industries.

The nature of industry in the modern age has other implications. Not only are components shipped with greater ease, but economic activity can physically move, in many cases to avoid the burdens of trade restrictions. During the 1980s, foreign automobile manufacturers established assembly operations in the United States in large part to come within the barriers established to protect the domestic manufacturers. When domestic manufacturers of flat-panel computer displays brought a dumping case against Japanese imports, U.S. computer firms intimated that they would move their assembly operations abroad, outside the protective barrier, to maintain their access to flat-panel displays on a par with their competitors. For reasons that, at least nominally, had nothing to do with this threat, the relief requested by the domestic industry was granted, but only in part, excluding the imports with the lightest volume. Some trade analysts question whether the trade laws operated appropriately in these cases; some question whether the trade laws were applied correctly, and others suggest that the ultimate results underscore the futility of the regulatory effort in the first place.

These issues may yet reach the logical extreme in the so-called Information Age. Information knows no political boundaries. As the nation-state of Kuwait fell, a Kuwaiti bank manager faxed the bank's records abroad and established operations in Bahrain. The bank opened the next day as a Bahraini financial institution, safe from both the Iraqi invaders and the accompanying U.S. freeze on Kuwaiti assets. Bolstered by technology, the burgeoning service sector is relatively free to cross international boundaries. Economists and statisticians have only begun to consider how to measure this trade, much less how it can be regulated in a free society. Trade officials have only marginally begun to consider how to deal with this important segment of the economy.

Many issues that surround trade regulation today can be catalogued under two general headings: one relating to substance, the other to procedure. The substantive category is this: What ultimate goals should international trade regulations serve? Typically, those labeled free traders argue in favor of a generally recognized definition of economic efficiency or consumer welfare. Those labeled protectionists place primary importance on general economic activity within the United States, measured in such terms as onshore manufacturing, domestic employment, and employment of domestic capital. As developed in the following chapters, the international trade laws do not necessarily reflect a consistent hierarchy of goals, and, in some cases, amendments to the trade laws have obscured the original intentions over time.

To what extent should those responsible for making decisions in international trade cases have the discretion to interpret the laws or to craft remedies that take account of evolving economic conditions such as those described above? Once again, different international trade laws differ on this point. The extent to which a regulatory body has discretion not only permits the regulator to apply the laws in ways that accommodate new circumstances; it also grants the regulator some authority to choose the goals that the regulation will achieve. Over the years, therefore, trade laws have tended to restrict the regulators' discretion and thus reflected congressional dissatisfaction with the goals and methods chosen by administrators. This practice emanates from the continuing battle between Congress and the executive branch for primacy in trade matters, with the executive seeking the maximum degree of flexibility and Congress taking steps to ensure that its agenda is followed.

This volume does not provide the answers to these questions. The literature on these issues is enormous, as are the accumulated materials on the economic and legal theories underlying trade policy and regulation. No small volume, and probably no single volume of any size, could give an accurate picture of the complexity and breadth of issues daily confronting those involved in trade policy.

Instead, the purpose of this volume is to explain the day-to-day mechanisms by which international trade decisions are made: the second category of issues. This procedural system reflects the sum of the legislative and regulatory response to these issues. If the goals of the trade regulations in this country are revealed anywhere, they should be revealed in the substance of the regulations in practice. Any flexibility to address new circumstances or to achieve new goals in changing conditions will be revealed in the mechanics of the process.

I am of the view that the international trade laws of this country are in need of reform. In many cases, the trade laws are based on antiquated premises, have lost sight of their original goals, and do not provide the flexibility needed to address new situations. Many international trade laws are both overinclusive and underinclusive; that is, they impose sanctions on legitimate and beneficial activity, while leaving unimpeded activity that should, at least according to the premises on which the regulation is based, fall within the regulatory scope. Some of the laws should be abolished, some modified, some kept substantially as they are.

I have tried to exclude these views from the following chapters. By setting forth the gist of the trade laws, procedures, agencies, and mechanisms that drive U.S. trade policy on a day-to-day basis, I hope that others will have the basic tools necessary to follow and participate in the trade debate beyond the misapplied labels. This book explains the problems that these laws purport to address, the procedures by which the decisions are made, and the extent to which the decision makers are free to craft solutions to the specific problems before them. At the least, I intend to provide an overview of the trade system in place today, so that the issues raised by the international trade system will be clearer and the overblown rhetoric and misleading labels can be set aside.

2
A History of U.S. Trade Policy

International trade and investment have been important factors in American political and economic affairs since the eighteenth century. The Acts of Parliament that catalyzed the American Revolution were, after all, trade barriers. The "taxation" referred to in the slogan "no taxation without representation" consisted of tariffs and other excise taxes. The Declaration of Independence cited Britain for cutting off American trade "with all parts of the World."

The history of U.S. policy regarding international trade since the Revolution provides a useful context for the current trade laws. International trade as an important political issue of recent years is not an aberration, but a return to the status quo interrupted by a temporary hiatus after World War II. History shows the evolution of international trade policy from a reliance on tariffs as a source of federal government revenue and industrial protection to a series of trade remedies targeted at particular conduct in international markets.

Early Issues

The early days following adoption of the Constitution were rife with controversy over the tariff question. The Federalists and the Jeffersonian Democrats differed over much, but perhaps not more than over questions of foreign commerce. Jefferson, Madison, and their fellow southern planters generally favored a more liberal trade policy. Hamilton ardently favored a protectionist policy designed to foster the growth of infant domestic manufacturing industries. In Hamilton's view, a protective tariff was intended to maintain a domestic monopoly for local manufacturers. Events went Hamilton's way. French and English trade restrictions adopted during the Napoleonic Wars (along with British conscription) drew even the Madison administration into a series of retaliatory countermeasures. Ultimately, the United States was drawn into the War of 1812. The lessons of that conflict reinforced the young republic's already hard-ened aversion to foreign political entanglements and added a strong measure of economic isolationism, particularly regarding Europe.

Even before the war, however, no real sentiment in the United States favored what would today be called free trade. Among other things, tariffs were a practical necessity. Because the Constitution in that day prohibited direct taxation that was not proportional to state population, an income tax was a practical impossibility—not to mention an eighteenth-century administrative nightmare. The fed-eral government depended on tariffs for a substantial part of its rev-enues until the early twentieth century. Debate over tariffs thus centered on the adoption of a high protective tariff or a lower rev-enue tariff designed to fund the government, with a minimum of intrusion on foreign commerce.

A powerful eighteenth-century political philosophy, endorsed by the Whig Party and then by the Republicans, was known as the American System: a focused drive west funded by government im-provements and commercial development behind a protective tariff wall. Opposition to the American System or to similar policies was sporadic. South Carolina generated an early constitutional crisis when it proposed to nullify a new tariff measure enacted in 1832 (both sides backed down the following year). After a respite in the 1840s—when tariff reductions increased federal revenues enough to cover the public debt incurred during the Mexican War—import barriers again rose. The Republican victory in 1860 heralded that party's political dominance and a return to higher tariff rates for half a century. The tariffs adopted to generate revenues to pay for the Civil War were set at high levels unprecedented since the "tariff of abominations" thirty years earlier.

The debate over the tariff question escalated during the 1890s. Tariffs were a key factor in each of the presidential races and con-gressional races of this period. The McKinley Tariff of 1890 set the standard. Progressive forces led by Grover Cleveland could not bring about immediate reductions when they were in power. Tariffs would fluctuate around the McKinley benchmark until the end of World War I.

Several provisions of the McKinley Tariff Act broke new ground in trade policy and presaged the shape of trade relations in the twen-tieth century. The president was authorized to enter into trade ne-gotiations with other countries with an eye to reducing tariffs on a reciprocal basis. Another provision lowered or eliminated duties in certain tropical agricultural products but empowered the president to impose duties on imports from countries that maintained "unjust or unreasonable" barriers to U.S. exports. The statute barred the importation of goods made by conscripts. The act thus introduced into modern tariff legislation the notions that trade measures could be used flexibly to open foreign markets and that sanctions could be targeted at particular conduct in international markets rather than against imports of whatever origin or character.

The tariff legislation was enacted in March 1897. Congress increased tariffs and authorized another round of reciprocal tariff negotiations, directed at both South America and certain European countries. The statute also called for the imposition of special tariffs, or countervailing duties, on imports that benefited from foreign government bounties, or subsidies. The countervailing duty scheme in current law, described in chapter 4, is a stepchild of this early measure.

A New Century

The new century saw the introduction of a "scientific" tariff. Such a tariff would not be set by political forces but rather would have a rational economic foundation. Republicans championed a version of this tariff that would equalize the difference in the cost of production (including a reasonable profit) for a U.S. industry and its foreign competitors. The Democratic Party, which linked Republican high-tariff policies with support for the trusts, made a similar proposal called a competitive tariff, which placed less emphasis on profit.

In 1909, Congress revisited the issue of tariffs. The law featured a new approach to tariff formulation and prepared for subsequent administrative reform. The law permitted the president to impose a tariff of 25 percent on top of existing tariffs on imports from countries that "unduly discriminate[d]" against the United States. President Taft, however, minimized the use of the penalty.

Woodrow Wilson adhered to the populist doctrine that linked tariffs and trusts. Although he pushed a tariff-reduction bill through Congress in 1913, tariffs had been set at such a high level that the reductions had little effect on trade or revenue. While Wilson made headway in tariff reduction, his imprint came in other areas that had an indirect, but substantial, impact.

First, in 1916, the states ratified the Sixteenth Amendment to the Constitution, which permitted the federal government to impose a direct income tax. Pressure on the government to finance operations through tariffs and domestic excise taxes eased. From that point on, the tariff question became exclusively an issue of industrial policy, without raising complicated questions of public finance.

The seeds of the administrative state were planted during this era. In 1916, President Wilson proposed and Congress established the Tariff Commission (now the U.S. International Trade Commission) to examine and advise on the development of equitable tariffs. Much of the commission's early work consisted of investigations into the relative costs of producing articles and the recommendation of corresponding tariff levels. The agency also recommended changes in the administration of customs, many of which were adopted.

Finally, that same year, Congress added a provision to the U.S. antitrust laws prohibiting predatory dumping, that is, the systematic sale of imported articles in the United States at substantially less than their fair market value, with the intent to injure, destroy, or prevent the establishment of a U.S. industry. In light of the difficulties in establishing intent and the greater likelihood of import relief from other remedies, the 1916 antidumping statute has rarely been invoked—and never successfully.

Congress amended this statute in 1921 with a major change in trade policy independent of a tariff statute. Following a Tariff Commission study critical of the 1916 antidumping measure, Congress established an administrative dumping remedy that forms the nucleus of the current U.S. system. That provision called on the secretary of the Treasury to impose duties on imported goods sold at "less than fair value" in the United States. These provisions were ultimately codified in the Tariff Act of 1930, which became the statutory platform for all subsequent amendments to the trade laws.

In 1922, Congress passed a law barring unfair trade practices in international trade. The language mirrored the operative language in the statute that created the Federal Trade Commission. While that legislation has been used primarily for consumer protection and antitrust activity, the successor to the 1922 trade provision (section 337 of the Tariff Act of 1930, discussed in chapter 6) has been used mostly by U.S. intellectual property owners to bar infringement. Efforts to expand the reach of this statute have been unsuccessful, not because of apparent legal barriers primarily, but because of presidential reluctance to expand the statute's reach beyond accepted bounds.

For more than sixty years, the Tariff Act of 1930 (Smoot-Hawley Tariff Act) has been widely considered one of the grave economic and political errors of the twentieth century. Recently, new and controversial analyses argue that the statute's impact has been overstated. But certain facts are indisputable: effective tariff rates following the 1930 act were as high as or higher than any in the previous one hundred years, and the volume of international trade subsequently collapsed as a result of tariffs and other factors. The Smoot-Hawley era was the last in which major trading nations imposed a system of new tariff barriers on international trade during peacetime.

The Roosevelt administration, as part of its general reaction to the Great Depression, established an agenda for reviving international trade in the Reciprocal Trade Agreements Act of 1934. That statute granted the president broad authority to enter into agreements with other nations (subject to congressional approval) for the mutual reduction of tariff barriers. The trade agreements rested on twin pillars: (1) reciprocity, so that tariffs were reduced on a bilateral basis, and (2) most-favored-nation treatment, so that the benefits of an agreement had a multiplicative effect on every nation that was a party to one agreement. While these principles had been used in the past, they had not been deployed on so comprehensive and expansive a basis.

Not surprisingly, in light of the economic devastation in Europe and Asia, the trends in American trade policy became the foundation for the multilateral trade regime established after World War II. But the modern era began with a resounding defeat. In 1947–1948, a multinational conference established a charter for an International Trade Organization (ITO), which was to be the third pillar of the international economic structure formed by the World Bank and the International Monetary Fund. The U.S. Senate, however, refused to adopt this so-called Havana Charter, and no formal trade structure existed for nearly fifty years.

GATT

In the view of many observers, most notably former diplomat, academic, and corporate counsel Kenneth Dam, that defeat was the source of the international trade system's current strength. The measure that filled the gap is simple enough. During the preparation of the Havana Charter, a group of nations, including the United States, prepared a preliminary protocol on substantive trade matters. With the demise of the ITO, the signatories agreed to abide by this second agreement. The protocol of provisional application became the nucleus of the General Agreement on Tariffs and Trade. In 1948, President Truman approved U.S. participation in the GATT. Congress has implemented the provisions of the original GATT and subsequent amendments, although it never ratified the agreement itself.

The GATT's success stems from several interrelated aspects of its character. It has no formal institutional structure. The agreement had a small, highly regarded secretariat headquartered in Geneva. Its council comprised representatives of all members and was operated by consensus. The GATT could become whatever its expanding membership agreed it should become. While at times frustrating efforts to adopt significant reforms, this feature ensured that the agreements reached had universal support among all participants. The GATT has literally molded itself to its role.

Substantively, too, the GATT benefited from ITO's failure. While the Havana Charter delved into various aspects of the signatories' economic relations, the GATT focused on only one element: the elimination of nontariff barriers to trade and the progressive reduction of tariffs by mutual assent. From this narrow substantive base, the GATT was able to expand incrementally in a fashion that was (and, under GATT operating procedures, had to be) acceptable to all signatories.

Operationally, the GATT called on signatories to enter into mutual concessions on tariff rates. Once a party made a concession, the tariff was bound and could not be raised again. Negotiations to lower tariffs were conducted during periodic rounds, or negotiation sessions, in which parties made what were, at least initially, a series of bilateral arrangements under the auspices of a multilateral forum.

The GATT rested on two fundamental principles. The first was nondiscrimination. With few exceptions, any signatory had to provide equivalent benefits, concessions, and terms of trade to all GATT signatories. The second was a most-favored-nation requirement: each signatory was entitled to the most beneficial terms offered by any other signatory. By virtue of these provisions, bilateral concessions among signatories had a multiplicative effect on trade because they automatically applied to all of the signatories alike.

The GATT provided exceptions to its basic provisions for extraordinary circumstances. An escape clause permitted signatories to raise tariffs or establish quotas in cases of "serious injury" to a domestic industry as a result of a tariff concession. The occasional use of domestic law implementing the escape clause has not had any substantial effect on trade. As one example, however, of a trade law that has lost its original moorings, the U.S. version of the escape clause no longer links relief to injury caused by a tariff concession. The escape clause as codified in U.S. law is discussed in chapter 5.

Over the course of five decades, the GATT hosted a series of rounds of multilateral trade negotiations. Between 1947 and 1970, GATT members participated in six rounds. The consequence of these negotiations was the dramatic reduction of tariff levels, particularly among industrialized nations. The extent of these transactions is revealed by a comparison with earlier activities. Between 1934 and 1947, the United States negotiated trade concessions on a bilateral basis with thirty-two countries under the Reciprocal Trade Agreements Act. The United States negotiated with twenty-two countries during the first GATT round alone and was the beneficiary (under the most-favored-nations clause) of the bilateral arrangements between other member-countries.

Between these countries, the level of tariffs in most commodities fell to a level that was nearly insignificant in commercial terms. By 1970, the ratio of all duties collected by the United States to the value of all imports was about 6.5 percent, and the ratio of duties collected to the value of dutiable imports was about 10 percent. In comparison, even before the Smoot-Hawley Tariff Act, tariff levels were often 30 percent of the value of imports—or even higher.

The reduction in tariffs elevated the importance of other trade barriers, such as discriminatory domestic regulations, oppressive customs procedures, subsidies for domestic manufacturers (both domestic subsidies and export subsidies), industrial organizations that formally or informally limited commercial opportunities for foreign producers, licensing and standards requirements, health measures, and even cultural barriers to imported products. During the 1960s, the GATT increasingly turned its attention to these issues, even as it continued to reduce tariffs.

The original GATT text addressed many nontariff trading practices but usually in only a cursory fashion. Dumping, for example, was "condemned," and Article 5 of the original GATT text contained provisions about antidumping duties. But high tariff rates meant that there was little need for a detailed assessment of dumping activity or procedures. The escape clause and other provisions related directly to tariff issues (such as customs procedures or preferential trading areas) received much greater attention during these early years.

Nontariff matters received more attention during the Kennedy Round of trade negotiations, which ended in 1969, but the efforts met with little success. The GATT signatories formulated a detailed dumping code that addressed both the substantive and the procedural aspects of the administration of domestic dumping laws. While the signatories agreed, the U.S. Congress did not. Under the GATT rules, a country could not be bound by an agreement to which it did not formally accede. The dumping code collapsed without American participation.[1]

One of the most significant GATT rounds was the Tokyo Round of the 1970s. While the Tokyo Round resulted in a significant drop in tariff levels (U.S. duties dropped by about 50 percent as a percentage of total imports during the period 1970–1992), the magnitude of the drop was only five percentage points. The historical importance of the Tokyo Round was the emphasis the parties placed on the adoption of codes governing nontariff trade practices.

The nations agreed to a subsidies code that addressed allowed government subsidies and the imposition of countervailing duties in other cases and to a dumping code that specified the standards and administrative procedures in domestic dumping cases. Most important, these codes established an injury test: no antidumping or countervailing duties could be imposed without an independent determination that a domestic industry had been harmed by the trade practice at issue. The U.S. Congress adopted legislation implementing the codes, although the codes were clearly not self-executing— in the event of a conflict between the code provisions and U.S. law, the latter would apply. These codes and the 1979 legislation implementing them form the foundation of the two most significant U.S. trade remedies in force today.

The GATT as an institution ceased to exist in 1995. That year the World Trade Organization (WTO) succeeded to the GATT's role in international commerce. In most respects, the WTO charter merely codifies the administrative procedures and informal practices developed under the GATT. The WTO was the achievement of an extraordinary eight-year trade negotiation known as the Uruguay Round. In addition to the traditional tariff negotiations (now dubbed market access talks) and the discussions on the establishment of the ITO and its charter, the Uruguay Round included on its agenda two items that will leave an important mark on the world economy of the twenty-first century.

World Trade Organization

The GATT agreement formally established the World Trade Organization. This body replaced the provisional GATT and is the permanent multilateral trade body envisioned nearly fifty years earlier. Originally entitled the Multilateral Trade Organization, it was renamed at the urging of the United States. This new organization replaces the GATT secretariat and administers the trading rules. It is headed by Renato Ruggierio of Italy as its first director general. Trade laws, regulations, and practices of WTO members are monitored by the Trade Policy Review Body. In addition to this monitoring function, the body can make recommendations to WTO members regarding trade practices.

Another difference in the WTO format was the requirement that member-countries agree to all GATT agreements. Before the end of the Uruguay Round, GATT member-countries were free to ratify particular GATT agreements or not. Only twenty-three GATT members, for example, were signatories to the GATT Agreement on Government Procurement. Similarly, GATT member-countries were free to join GATT codes on subsidies and countervailing measures and so on. This a la carte format weakened the multilateral trading system and made results of trade disputes less predictable. In a countervailing duty case involving two GATT members, for example, the question of whether an injury analysis was required hinged on whether the offending state was also a signatory of the GATT code on subsidies.

The earlier model also created substantial free-rider problems. The relaxation of trade barriers benefited all trading partners. Nonsignatory states still received some benefit from GATT agreements. An additional gain from the all-inclusive GATT strategy is the possibility of cross-retaliation. Assume that the United States and Benin are engaged in a trade dispute regarding the latter's failure to protect U.S. intellectual property. The United States could not effectively retaliate against Benin by imposing sanctions on patented works from Benin. Instead, the United States would seek to retaliate against imports of specific goods from Benin, such as textiles. If Benin were not a member of the GATT code on intellectual property, it might argue that this cross-sectoral retaliation was inappropriate.

Before the Uruguay Round, cross-sectoral retaliation was not consistent within the GATT.

After the Uruguay Round, WTO members must become signatories of all WTO agreements. Member-states must also make binding commitments to lower trade barriers according to an agreed schedule.

Trade Disputes and the WTO

The WTO has a significant role in settling trade disputes among members. The decisions of the dispute resolution panels, however, are not binding interpretations of the GATT agreement.

One earlier criticism of the GATT and GATT dispute settlement centered on the ability of parties to block the decisions of arbitral panels. A GATT panel, for example, concluded that U.S. protection of intellectual property under section 337 denied national treatment (that is, nonpreferential treatment to domestic products) to imports. The United States, like any other GATT member, had the ability to block acceptance of the report and did so five times. GATT members could also seek and receive waivers of various GATT obligations. The WTO granted waivers to some states, but a more stringent standard is envisioned for future waivers. Three-fourths of all WTO members must approve future waivers from GATT rules or dispute panel determinations. Hypothetically, if a state such as Burundi requested a waiver from a phase-in obligation such as patent protection, that request would require the unanimous approval of all WTO members.

The WTO improves on the GATT by adding trade in services to its authority. The global market for services is valued at $3.9 trillion. Included with the services sectors are construction, engineering, accounting and professional services, and computer services. Sectors where the United States has large trade surpluses such as health care, environmental services, education, and tourism are also part of the services sector. Inclusion of this sector with the WTO was particularly important to the United States and other western states.

A lack of member consensus kept financial services and audiovisual services from being covered by this agreement. They remain subjects of continuing WTO negotiations.

The inclusion of trade-related investment measures (TRIMS) within the WTO was also significant for the United States. By inclusion of TRIMS within the WTO framework, members agree to WTO policies of nondiscrimination against foreign investors. This provision, however, does not open all sectors of an economy to foreign investment. The United States, for example, still retains the ability to monitor foreign investment and deny foreign investment in certain industries such as nuclear power, maritime shipping, and broadcasting. Additional screening of foreign investment on national security grounds is still permitted under the Exon-Florio Act.

Another WTO agreement of paramount interest to the United States is the Agreement on Trade-Related Aspects of Intellectual Property Rights (TRIPS). This provision requires WTO members to protect and to develop measures of protecting intellectual property. Included within this agreement are patents, trademarks, copyrights, computer software, and chip masks. The agreement allows developing states to adopt protection of intellectual property gradually. This phase-in reflects the compromise between North and South. Industrialized WTO member-states with the most to lose from inadequate protection of intellectual property were unable to convince the developing and less developed WTO members to agree to immediate protection.

The WTO Agreement on Agriculture, another breakthrough measure, extended the scope of the WTO into trade in agricultural products. Most significant, pursuant to this agreement, WTO members agree to phase out agricultural export subsidies gradually. Members also apply the WTO doctrine of tariffication and replace quotas on agricultural products with less trade-distorting tariffs. This hard-fought provision was one of the most contentious in the Uruguay Round.

The Agreement on Government Procurement replaces the old, undersubscribed GATT code on government procurement. Under the new agreement, parties agree to clarify often byzantine national regulations. Additionally, states agree to apply WTO principles of national treatment to government procurement practices. Programs such as "Buy American" will be eliminated under this agreement, and most federal procurement will be opened to international competition.

Contrary to the criticism of some, the WTO cannot threaten U.S. sovereignty. First, the global trade organization has no enforcement powers. The GATT cannot rewrite U.S. laws or levy taxes on violators.

During the GATT debate, the Federation of Tax Administrators and the Multistate Tax Commission joined the cacophony of critics condemning the WTO. The tax officials argued that dispute panels of the WTO might "substitute WTO for the U.S. Supreme Court." These state officers were concerned that state taxing power would shift from state capitols to Geneva with any alterations requiring the assent and review of bureaucrats of the WTO.

Ralph Nader similarly warned the Senate Finance Committee that the WTO would "undermine citizen control and chill the ability of domestic democratic bodies to make decisions on a vast array of domestic policies from food safety to federal and state procurement to communications and foreign investment policies."

The WTO does not create new standards or call for any harmonization downward in standards. Like its predecessor, the WTO is first and foremost a forum for the resolution of trade disputes. States are still free to maintain different standards, even higher standards. The only difference is that these standards must be based on scientific standards and not be purely a pretext for protectionism. The WTO will not tell states what goals are worthwhile and which ones are not. Instead, the WTO is a multilateral sounding board to assess whether the least restrictive measures are being used.

Fortunately, leading constitutional law scholars have successfully debunked this idea. Former appeals court judge Robert Bork, one of our nation's most eminent constitutional law scholars, has concluded that "the sovereignty issue . . . is merely a scarecrow. Under our constitutional system, no treaty or international agreement can bind the United States if it does not wish to be bound. Congress may at any time override such an agreement or any provision of it by statute."

In addition, Professor John Jackson of the University of Michigan Law School, a leading GATT expert, joined in dismissing the loss of sovereignty claims as "ludicrous." Professor Jackson also concluded that "a careful examination of the WTO charter leads me to conclude that the WTO has no more real power than that which existed for the GATT under the previous agreements."

A hotly contested area of the sovereignty debate focused on the WTO mechanism to settle disputes. Pursuant to Article 23 of the GATT, members of the WTO are required to use its settlement procedures whenever they seek redress of a violation of obligations, other nullification, or impairment. Members are to "abide by the rules and procedures of this understanding."

Critics of this agreement contended that section 301 will be scrapped in favor of WTO's dispute settlement mechanism.[2] If the United States were to pursue an independent and unilateral course of retaliation while ignoring the GATT, this action would be inconsistent with Article 23.

The United States, however, is not required to submit to Article 23, WTO's procedure for settlement. During legislative debate on the GATT, members of Congress were careful not to abandon their option for unilateral action. Legislation for implementation of the GATT specifically states that "no provision of any of the Uruguay Round Agreements, nor the application of any such provision to any person or circumstance, that is inconsistent with any law of the United States shall have effect." Further, "nothing in this Act shall be construed (A) to amend or modify any law of the United States, including any law relating to limit any authority conferred under any law of the United States, including Section 301 of the Trade Act of 1974."[3] Similarly, as part of the price for approval of the GATT, Congress has been debating creation of a WTO dispute panel review board. This commission of five federal judges would review decisions of a WTO dispute panel against the United States. This review would determine if the WTO panel in these cases "demonstrably exceeded its authority," acted "arbitrarily or capriciously," or "added to the obligations, or diminished the rights of, the United States under the Uruguay Round Agreement."[4] If the federal judicial commission issued three affirmative reports in a five-year period, any member of Congress could institute a resolution calling for U.S. withdrawal from the WTO.

U.S. Trade in the Present

Where does the United States stand at this moment? As mentioned, the GATT has succeeded in eliminating tariffs as a significant commercial factor in international trade, at least as far as most products are concerned. In 1992, even before the Uruguay Round and NAFTA tariff reductions, only about 37 percent of U.S. imports came in duty free; this figure suggests that the tariffs imposed on the other 63 percent were not a substantial barrier to trade. In fact, the ratio of the value of the tariffs collected on U.S. imports to the total value of dutiable imports was only about 5 percent that year. The ratio of duties to total imports was about 3 percent. The data for other industrialized countries were on the same order of magnitude. Continued work will undoubtedly take place in this area, but the importance of tariff barriers among the major trading nations has been marginalized.

The contentious issue with which the United States and other signatories to the WTO will have to grapple in the immediate future is whether countries with different economic systems can trade under a system of open markets and, if so, on what terms. The irony is that this question has been raised most often in the United States regarding two of its largest export markets, Japan and Mexico. Japan, it is said, maintains cultural, legal, and commercial barriers to U.S. exports that cannot be remedied by targeted tariffs, such as the antidumping or countervailing duty remedies. While Japan has been a frequent target of traditional trade cases particularly in the dumping area, it has also been the target of separate bilateral arrangements regarding specific industrial markets (automobiles, semiconductors) and certain categories of trade practices (such as the so-called *keiretsu* system of industrial organization).

As to Mexico, the argument runs that the different levels of economic development in the two countries, manifested by large wage differentials and widely disparate levels of commercial regulation, are barriers to fair trade between the two countries. "Social dumping" in the form of low wage rates and lax regulations in such areas as environmental controls and child labor laws, it is said, are issues beyond the current trade regime.

In large measure, these developments show that the international trading system developed in this century is a victim of its own success. Whether the system can withstand the storms that rage about it is questionable. Several important issues are at hand. In the case of Mexico, the United States induced the NAFTA signatories to append side agreements relating to labor and environment issues. With regard to Japan (and other countries), the United States has made extensive use of its controversial section 301 procedures (discussed in chapter 9), a procedure so controversial that it alone brought the trade system to the brink of collapse in early 1995. The use of section 301 will almost certainly be addressed in WTO negotiations. Talk is also in the air of a new WTO competition code to address industrial organization issues like *keiretsu* and possibly even pricing issues and to replace the current dumping code.

In summary, little is gained by the use of name-calling or labels in the international trade context. One might or might not approve of the regulatory regime that has come to replace the system of tariffs—at least tariffs had the twin virtues of certainty and simplicity. Tariffs also worked through the price system. A particularly efficient exporter may overcome many negative impacts of tariffs. In the current context, arguing about more or less protection is almost futile. The most pertinent issue is how trade is regulated and whether the regulatory system achieves reasonable goals that have been set for it.

3
Antidumping

Perhaps no international trade concept is more frequently discussed, and more frequently misunderstood, than dumping. As defined in the GATT and U.S. trade law, dumping is the sale of a product in an export market at a price that is either below the price at which the product is sold in the manufacturer's home market or a comparable third-country market or below the product's cost of manufacture. Consequently, the antidumping law covers both more and less than efforts by foreign manufacturers to undercut domestic industries by underselling domestic products: the law can result in duties on imports that are sold at prices designed only to meet (or, in some cases, to establish) a competitive price in the U.S. market, while it neglects entirely certain economic and industrial strategies by foreign firms and their governments that can result in hypercompetitive pressure on a U.S. industry. As shown below, the dumping law reflects a complex balance of competing tendencies, such as protectionism and politics.

Price Discrimination and Predation

In most instances, dumping occurs when a seller engages in price discrimination on international markets. A French perfume producer dumps when it sells the identical product for $100 an ounce in New York and $150 an ounce in Paris. In theory, a producer could engage in reverse dumping by selling a product at a higher price in its export market than in its home market. Reverse dumping, like dumping itself, can occur at any given time, as a result of factors such as fluctuations in exchange rates or changing market conditions that result in price movements in one country. Not surprisingly, even if reverse dumping occurs on a systematic basis, it rarely becomes a contentious issue.

Why would a producer dump intentionally? To the extent that a producer can engage in price discrimination, dumping maximizes revenues. By selling at price X, a producer loses customers who would purchase the offered product at a lower price that still covers production costs. The producer also sells to customers who would pay more than X. Transaction costs aside, the producer that could negotiate with every customer the price of every unit sold would generate more revenue than a producer that charges all consumers a single price.

A second-best approach to maximizing revenue is to discriminate in different markets. A producer that takes this approach sets the price higher where demand is high, where the commodity is considered a luxury, or where other market factors make a high price sustainable. In markets where the high price is not sustainable, the producer lowers the price to meet market conditions. Regional price discrimination within a large national market is not unusual and in most instances is perfectly legal.

Price discrimination on international markets has additional implications. First, discrimination is sustainable only when a barrier to trade prevents arbitrage between two markets in which a price differential exists. Absent a trade barrier, arbitrageurs will buy in the market where the price is low and sell in the market where the price is high, until the prices are at relative parity. The trade barriers to effective arbitrage may be as innocuous as transportation costs. They may also include tariffs or quotas, regulations that favor domestic products, informal customs policies and procedures, and restrictive licensing arrangements. Sustained dumping with no arbitrage may therefore be a symptom of unfair trade barriers between markets.

Second, dumping may entail selling a product below the cost of producing it. If used to undermine competition in the target market, then such predatory pricing is a violation of U.S. antitrust laws. Economists question whether a manufacturer can sustain predatory pricing over the long run in the face of existing potential competition in a national market with low barriers to entry. Scenarios have been described, however, in which a manufacturer that enjoys monopoly profits in a market protected by trade barriers benefits from selling additional units abroad, even below cost. In industries where large production runs lower the average cost of producing each unit, for example, selling below cost in a foreign market may result in an increase in total profits.

The dumping laws do not specifically address these issues. The law neither requires, as a condition for relief, that a foreign producer be engaged in predatory practices behind trade barriers nor addresses various other means available for engaging in unfair competition on international markets. Rather, the dumping law is addressed at a particular set of circumstances involving price discrepancies or below-cost selling in different markets. The development of the dumping laws and the way the law functions in practice are described below.

The Evolution of the Dumping Laws

During the period around World War I, manufacturers in several countries—particularly German chemical companies—were organized as protective cartels. From this privileged industrial base, these firms presented daunting competition for U.S. manufacturers, even in the U.S. market.

In some cases in direct response to the threat from these cartels, several countries passed laws outlawing predatory pricing on international markets. In the United States, Congress enacted the Antidumping Act of 1916 as part of the antitrust laws. The 1916 statute outlaws the sale of an imported product in the United States at a predatory price with the intention of injuring a U.S. firm. As with the other antitrust laws, the 1916 statute provides for an award of damages to the successful plaintiff. The specific elements of a claim under the statute, particularly the requirement that the plaintiff show that the producer had a specific intention to injure a U.S. firm, however, makes proving a claim under the 1916 act onerous.

In response to criticism of the 1916 act on these grounds, Congress asked the Tariff Commission (now the International Trade Commission) to consider the matter and make recommendations for changes in the law. The commission reported that the burden of demonstrating a foreign producer's specific intent was too high a hurdle for a plaintiff to overcome reasonably. Citing the practice in other countries, particularly Canada, the commission suggested that Congress establish an administrative trade remedy for unfairly priced imports.

The result was the Antidumping Act of 1921, which Congress later incorporated into the Tariff Act of 1930. Under the antidumping act, a domestic industry could petition the Treasury Department to impose duties on imported goods to offset price discrimination. The act did not require that the imports be sold below cost or that the price discrimination be supported by an unfair barrier to trade.

The administrative remedy was available upon a demonstration of international price discrimination alone. Subsequently, Congress added the requirement that the petition show injury to a domestic industry, and this requirement was adopted in international practices and codified in the GATT antidumping code. Thus, while the 1916 act requires a showing of injury to domestic *competition*, the 1921 act and subsequent incarnations of the dumping laws require a showing of injury to *competitors*.

Domestic industries found stark differences in the usefulness of the 1916 and the 1921 antidumping laws. No plaintiff has successfully brought a claim under the 1916 act. In fact, few even attempted to do so. Conversely, according to ITC statistics, between 1980 and 1993, 682 antidumping cases were filed in the United States under the 1921 antidumping act, and 39 percent of them resulted in affirmative final determinations.

Although many basic features of the antidumping law can be traced to the original 1921 statute, the law has been amended many times. Most recently, the law was amended in 1994 (to be effective in 1995) to reflect the agreements reached on dumping issues during the Uruguay Round negotiations. While many changes were technical and their ultimate impact on administration of the law is uncertain, they do reflect the further evolution of and refinement of the antidumping laws.

The pertinent sections of the dumping law provide that (1) if the "administering authority determines that a class or kind of foreign merchandise is being or is likely to be sold in the United States at less than fair value" and (2) "the Commission determines that an industry in the United States is materially injured or threatened with material injury, or the establishment of an industry in the United States is materially retarded by reason of imports of that merchandise," then "there shall be imposed on such merchandise an antidumping duty, in addition to any other duty imposed, in an amount equal to the amount by which the normal value exceeds the export price of the merchandise." The Commerce Department, as the designated administering authority, conducts an investigation to determine whether dumping is taking, or is likely to take, place. The "Commission" is the International Trade Commission, which considers the question of injury.

The calculation of dumping margins—the extent to which goods in the United States are sold at less than fair value and the basis on which antidumping duties are assessed—is one of the most technically complex procedures in international trade regulation. In any given case, a judgment on an accounting issue or the Commerce Department's adoption of a particular approach to a calculation can have a material impact on the size of the margin. High margins, even margins in the triple digits, are not uncommon.

Rarely, however, will Commerce actually conclude that no dumping has occurred. Several reasons relating to Commerce's traditional calculations can be cited as a cause. As discussed below, a few of these points have been addressed in the most recent amendments to the statute. The reason also goes to the heart of the law itself. The dumping laws, for example, do not have a "meeting the competition" defense (as the related U.S. antitrust laws do). Consequently, a dumping finding means not that imports are anticompetitive but only that competitive conditions in two markets differ—hardly a surprising result.

Other critics would counter, however, that the law is not a domestic regulation but an international trade remedy directed to a particular practice deemed unfair by international trade standards. U.S. industry (the argument runs) is at a long-term disadvantage if competition in different markets is not level, and dumping would not occur on a systematic basis if markets were equally open and competitive. In large part, the two perspectives on which much of the political and academic debate on dumping centers, are whether dumping actually constitutes unfair trade and whether the dumping laws as adopted in the United States are an effective countermeasure.

These different views of the dumping law have seeped into judicial decisions as well. In a seminal case, the U.S. court of appeals for the federal circuit, which oversees dumping determinations, noted that

> Congress sought to afford the domestic manufacturer strong protection against dumping, seeming to indicate that the Secretary [of Commerce] should err in favor of protectionism. . . . On the other hand, the Secretary is directed to make a fair and equitable valuation, which may reduce the antidumping margin as a result of downward adjustments to foreign market value.[1]

The Court of International Trade, in a charitable response to this comment from its appellate court, suggested that "these two purposes of the statute complement, rather than conflict with each other," as the statute is clearly "designed to protect domestic indus-

tries from unfair trade practices of their competitors, while providing freedom for fair trade."[2] The extent to which this distinction is
achieved depends on the methodologies employed by the two agencies charged with enforcing the law.

The Dumping Investigation

The Petition. A dumping case typically begins when a producer representing a domestic industry or a union representing workers in a
domestic industry files a petition with the Commerce Department
and the ITC.[3] The petition must show, based on information reasonably available, that a "class or kind" of merchandise imported into
the United States is sold at less than fair value (LTFV). The petition
must also provide information showing that a domestic industry is
materially injured or threatened with material injury or that the development of a domestic industry is retarded by the imports. A typical petition will therefore describe the domestic industry and the
imported product, the pricing structure for the imported product in
the United States and in the producer's home market, and the analysis on which the petitioner bases its injury claim.

The petition must show the basis on which the petitioner pur-
ports to represent the domestic industry at large. If the petitioner is
a trade association comprising most domestic manufacturers or a
labor union representing most of the industry's workers, standing
to bring the petition is not usually an issue. If the petitioner is one
firm or a local union, standing may not be clear. Traditionally, Commerce has accepted a petition if firms whose collective output represents a majority of domestic production do not register an affirmative
(written) objection to the petition. Recent amendments to the antidumping law prohibit this "consent by silence" approach and require an affirmative statement of support by members of the industry.

The description of the class or kind of merchandise defines the
scope of the investigation. Only those imports within the class or
kind will be considered during the investigation and affected by an
antidumping order. The scope of the investigation is therefore of
critical strategic importance. A petitioner will usually seek to tailor
the definition of class or kind so that the products facing the heavi-
est competition from imports are included, while the definition is
not so narrow that an antidumping order could be readily bypassed.
The scope of definition set out in note 4 is not atypical.[4]

When a petition is filed, the Commerce Department has twenty days in which to decide whether to accept it. In practice, representatives of petitioners usually consult with Commerce and ITC officials during the drafting of a petition. Rarely does a petition come as a surprise—either to the agencies or to the Washington rumor mill. As a consequence, the department rarely rejects a petition at this early stage. Once the agency accepts the petition, it and the questionnaire are served on respondents—the known importers and foreign manufacturers identified in the petition—and the Washington embassies of the countries whose products are named in the petition.

Following the initiation of an investigation, the responsibility for moving the investigation forward shifts back and forth between Commerce and the ITC: ITC preliminary determination, Commerce preliminary determination, Commerce final determination, ITC final determination. If the ITC issues a negative determination at any point, the case is closed. If Commerce issues a negative final determination, the case is closed. The two agencies' areas of inquiry are completely separate, however, so their investigations are conducted entirely separately, even though they overlap temporally.

According to the prescribed time lines, the ITC must issue its final determination—the last phase of the dumping procedure— within 245 days of the filing of a petition, although a complicated case or a case involving a substantial number of respondents may be extended during the Commerce phase by up to four months. All fact-finding and administrative proceedings in which the agencies and the private parties engage occur during this relatively short period. The procedure described below should therefore be viewed in fast-forward, as government employees, industry executives, lawyers, economists, technical consultants, and clerical staff collect and process mountains of information to determine whether an antidumping order should issue.

Participation in an investigation is limited to interested parties. These parties include foreign manufacturers of the imports under consideration, foreign exporters, relevant foreign trade associations, and their government; U.S. importers of the product at issue; any manufacturer, producer, wholesaler, or labor union in the industry engaged in the manufacture, production, or wholesale of the domestic product at issue; and a domestic trade association associated with the relevant industry. The identity of the interested parties and, in particular, the composition of the domestic industry that will be the subject of the ITC's investigation are as broad or as narrow as the product identified in the petition.

Until recently, the impact of a dumping petition on international trade went far beyond the assessment of dumping duties—in fact, final dumping duties might not be assessed for many years. Rather, much of the impact on trade resulted from the uncertainty that a dumping investigation could generate during the years between the completion of an investigation and the assessment of final duties. The onset of a dumping investigation results in the suspension of liquidation, that is, the final tabulation of the amount of duties owed on importation.

At the completion of an investigation, the law requires the Customs Service to collect estimated duties in the amount established during the investigation and based on the dumping margin. Customs then continues to collect estimated duties until Commerce at the request of the original petitioner, an importer, or an exporter conducts a review of each import transaction during the year preceding the request. At that time or, if no one asked for a review, at the expiration of the time for making such a request, Commerce assesses a final dumping rate, which in most cases can be higher or lower than the estimated rate. Customs then collects the duties assessed during the review—often long after the imports in question—and the dumping margin calculated during the review is used to establish the level of estimated duties until the next review. There is no set period for the termination of an antidumping order or for the completion of an administrative review of imports under such an order.

The uncertainty generated by this scheme, as well as the decades of proceedings precipitated by the initial investigation, was an important subject of negotiations during the Uruguay Round. The agreement reached during this round resulted in amending the process. Under current law, Commerce still conducts reviews but must complete them within eighteen months. At the fifth anniversary of the dumping order, both the ITC and Commerce must conduct an investigation to determine whether the antidumping order should be revoked. The order must be revoked unless Commerce determines that on repeal of the order dumping would be likely to recur and unless the ITC concludes that material injury to a domestic industry would likely result.

The impact of this new provision on the administration of the antidumping law is not clear. The statute provides, for example, that a finding of no dumping in administrative reviews during the preceding five years does not necessarily mean that dumping will not recur. But the statute does not call for periodic five-year reviews, but only specifies the one-time review at the fifth anniversary. If the order is not revoked at the end of the five-year period, therefore, the situation under the new statute will be indistinguishable from that under the old.

The Dumping Determination. Commerce's role is to determine whether the imports subject to investigation are sold in the United States at less than fair value. Fair market value is based on normal value, the actual price at which the product is sold in the respondent's home market. Dumping occurs when normal value exceeds the price charged in the United States for the same product. The dumping margin is equal to the difference expressed as a percentage of the U.S. price. Ideally, the process of assessing whether dumping has occurred and calculating a margin entails a comparison of two sales of an identical products, one in the United States and the other in the respondent's home market, at a similar time and at a comparable point in the stream of commerce in each country. Unfortunately, neither Commerce nor the individual company's accounting systems make such an approach easy. Commerce therefore uses approximations and proxies that (some say) are required out of administrative necessity or (others say) unfairly distort the dumping analysis.

Commerce conducts the factual portion of its investigation by submitting to the major manufacturers of the imported product a series of questionnaires seeking data about the products sold in the home and U.S. markets and data on each particular sale. In most instances, Commerce requests written responses for aggregate data and calculations but demands data concerning individual sales on computer tapes with data formatted according to Commerce's specifications. In many cases, Commerce cannot feasibly calculate a dumping margin for each foreign producer; it therefore designates an "all others" rate for companies that were not actually a part of the investigation.

A common issue in many appeals of Commerce determinations stems from a respondent's inability or unwillingness to provide the department with the data requested in the prescribed period or format. In such cases, Commerce is authorized to calculate a margin based on the facts. In practice, Commerce assesses two tiers of "facts available" rates. The first is assessed on firms that refuse to cooperate in the investigation. The rate has a punitive element, as it is usually based on unfavorable information (such as that in the petition) or on a high margin found in another investigation. Firms that cooperate in the investigation but cannot provide the information requested are assessed a more moderate rate based on information provided and on the rates assessed against cooperative firms that provided complete data.

The first issue addressed by Commerce in an investigation is the model match, a process designed to ensure that Commerce compares the prices associated with sales of the most similar products available. In this phase, Commerce compares the class or kind of imports defined in the petition with "like products" in the producer's home market. There is no problem when the product is a homogeneous commodity. The matter is more complicated when the product is more complex and is therefore more likely to be manufactured to meet the specific industry standards, government regulations, and consumer tastes in a particular market. In some cases, too, Commerce divides the class or kind of merchandise into separate categories and develops different matches for each. Commerce then tries to identify the two products that represent the closest match based on physical characteristics, cost, and sales.

The next issue that Commerce confronts is the basis on which normal value will be calculated. The preferred approach is to base normal value on sales in the producer's home market. Commerce will use the foreign manufacturer's sales in the home market unless the volume of those sales is less than 5 percent of sales to the U.S. market.

If those sales are insufficient in number, either because the producer just does not make that many home market sales or because sales below the producer's cost of production are excluded, then Commerce must look to an alternative means. If acceptable home market sales are too few in number, Commerce will ignore the respondent's home market sales and use instead the respondent's sales in a third market. In essence, Commerce will look to producer's sale of the merchandise most similar to the class or kind of merchandise at issue that is sold in a country with marketing and distribution systems most like those of the United States.

If these sales are still inadequate for a comparison, Commerce will calculate the constructed value of the merchandise in the home market. Constructed value is equal to the cost of manufacture (labor, materials, and fabrication costs); the general, selling, and administrative expense; and profit. Commerce must now use actual expense and profit as determined by the General Services Administration rather than floor values, but the department retains administrative flexibility over calculations of the actual amounts.

Once the Commerce Department has determined the appropriate basis for the normal value, it considers the appropriate basis for the U.S. price. The rule of thumb is that Commerce will use the first sale by the foreign manufacturer to an unaffiliated party for export to the United States. If that sale occurs in the country of manufacture—that is, the foreign manufacturer and the importer are not affiliated—then the price of the sale is known as the export price (until this year, it was the purchase price). If the sale occurs in the United States—that is, the importer is an affiliate of the foreign manufacturer, such as a related U.S. distributor—then the price is known as the constructed export price (formerly, the exporter's sales price, or ESP). When Commerce uses export price sales, fewer adjustments are involved in reaching a basis for comparison with normal value. In many cases, the department will establish separate export price and constructed export price margins and combine them to reach its final determination.

The court of appeals has summarized the goal of the Commerce determination:

> Foreign market value and United States price represent prices in different markets affected by a variety of differences in the chain of commerce by which the merchandise reached the export or domestic market. Both values are subject to adjustment in an attempt to reconstruct the price at a specific "common" point in the chain of commerce, so that value can be fairly compared on an equivalent basis. While the statute does not specify *where* in the chain of commerce price is constructed, the specific statutory adjustments appear to be an "f.o.b. foreign port" price.[5]

Other courts have suggested that the objective is to reconstruct an *ex factory* price, that is, the price of the product involved in the home market sale and the U.S. market sale as each leaves the factory gate. In any event, the goal is an apples-to-apples comparison of equivalent prices.

The U.S. price is adjusted to account for the unique expenses associated with U.S. sales. An adjustment is made (in this case to U.S. price and normal value) to account for differences in packing costs to the extent they are included in the price. U.S. taxes and duties are deducted, as are inland and foreign freight costs, insurance premiums, and storage, brokerage, inspection, and handling fees. A deduction is also made for any export tax or charge imposed by the country of export.

These adjustments are made whether the value is calculated on export price or on constructed export price (CEP). If the calculation is made on a CEP basis, additional deductions are made for indirect selling expenses incurred in the United States (such as the general sales and administration, advertising costs, and sales commissions), profits attributable to the U.S. operation, and any value added to the product itself in U.S. facilities before the sale to the unaffiliated customer.

The adjustments made to the home market price (or third market price, when used) fall roughly into one of five categories. The first two concern adjustments for different sales quantities (to account for discounts and the like) and differences in the physical characteristics of the merchandise. The third adjustment takes into account differences in the circumstances of sales, including (but not limited to) credit expense, commissions, warrantees, technical assistance, and advertising. The fourth reflects differences in the level of trade, if any. The final series of adjustments concerns shipping charges and taxes, including excise taxes rebated on the export of the good duties imposed at the border.

The Dumping Calculation. Once the parties have submitted the data on which Commerce bases its dumping calculations, the department begins preparation of a preliminary determination. At the end of the preliminary investigation, Commerce calculates and publishes a preliminary dumping margin. In some cases, Commerce holds a disclosure conference with individual parties to discuss the methodology used to determine its particular dumping rate.

Following the release of the preliminary dumping margin, the Commerce Department conducts an on-site verification of the data included in the foreign producer's submissions and an administrative hearing. In advance of the hearing, all interested parties, foreign and domestic, may submit briefs pointing out legal, factual, and computational errors in the preliminary determination. The hearing is usually informal and conducted by a senior Commerce Department official in the Office of Import Administration with extensive participation by other officials involved in or with supervisory authority over the investigation.

After the hearing and taking into account the parties' submissions, Commerce calculates the final dumping margins. Usually, Commerce issues a final determination listing the dumping margin for each respondent, an "all-others" rate for parties that have not participated in the investigation, a point-by-point discussion addressing each issue raised by the parties in their written submissions or at the administrative hearing, and Commerce's resolution of the issue.

The actual calculation of the dumping margin was another important issue addressed during the Uruguay Round. Previously, Commerce compared individual U.S. sales prices with an average of the home market sales prices. If prices fluctuated during the period of investigation, Commerce could have found dumping even if the prices in the U.S. and the home market matched on any given day; that is, according to an average home market price, some of the individual U.S. prices fell below that average, and Commerce reached an affirmative determination. No offsetting credit was given for U.S. sales at prices that were above the average price in the home market, although those sales would have lowered the margin if all U.S. sales were weighted together. In other words, U.S. sales above the average were given a zero dumping rate, rather than a negative dumping rate.

Under the amended law, Commerce has a choice in an investigation: it can compare either individual sales in each market or, preferably, averages in each market. If the department uses averages in each market, then sales with negative margins will offset positive margins on other sales. Comparing individual sales—which Commerce would probably not do in most cases—would reduce the effects that appeared under the old methodology as a result of price fluctuations during the investigation. Sales with negative margins, however, would not offset sales with positive margins under this sale-by-sale methodology. In administrative reviews, Commerce is still required to compare the home market average price with individual U.S. prices.

Several factors influence the department's selection of matching sales. Commerce looks for sales of the most similar products. If the products are identical, then no adjustment need be made for different physical characteristics. If the products are merely similar, a complicated cost adjustment must be made. If the products are too dissimilar, Commerce treats them as separate categories and seeks matches for each category. If the department cannot match a U.S. model with a foreign model, it is forced to base normal value on constructed value.

Commerce also matches sales made only in the ordinary course of trade. Sales of closeout merchandise or obsolete products are generally excluded, even if those sales are included in the producer's total business plan. Sales that are below cost because of high start-up expenses have been included in certain narrow circumstances, which expanded somewhat in the recent amendments.

Once Commerce has made the price comparison, it determines the total dollar amount of dumping. That is, for each sale in which the normal value exceeds the U.S. price, Commerce calculates the difference in dollar terms. It then aggregates these values and divides that figure by the total dollar volume of U.S. sales during the relevant period. The result, stated in percentage terms, is the dumping margin, which sets the rate for estimated duties on future imports until Commerce repeats the process during an administrative review. At that time it calculates an actual duty to be levied on subsequent sales made during the review period. A dumping margin below 2 percent—a so-called *de minimis* rate—is ignored in an investigation. In a review, however, the *de minimis* dumping margin is 0.5 percent.

Anticircumvention. In view of technological developments and the increasing transportability of parts and manufacturing processes (discussed in chapter 1), Congress in 1988 incorporated provisions into the antidumping law to prevent foreign manufacturers from bypassing antidumping orders. These anticircumvention provisions took several forms.

First, Congress made provisions for later-developed merchandise. Merchandise developed after the initiation of an investigation may be included within the scope of the antidumping order if, on balance, (1) it has the same general physical characteristics as the merchandise covered by the original order and is directed to the same consumer expectations; (2) the ultimate use of the original and later-developed product is the same; (3) the two products are sold through the same channels of trade; and (4) the later-developed merchandise is advertised and displayed in a manner similar to the original product.

Second, Commerce may include the imported components within the antidumping order if (1) merchandise sold in the United States is of the same class or kind as the merchandise subject to an antidumping order; (2) the merchandise is assembled in the United States (or in a third country not subject to an antidumping order) from parts or components produced in the country to which the antidumping order applies; (3) the process of assembly is minor or insignificant; and (4) the value added in the United States is small.

The determination regarding the inclusion of later-developed merchandise or products assembled in the United States (or a third country) within the dumping order is initiated by filing an application with the Commerce Department. Interested parties are entitled to participate. The features of an antidumping investigation—issuance of a questionnaire, release of a preliminary determination, etc. —are optional. No formal determination by the ITC is required, although the ITC must be consulted and may comment on the impact of including the product within its determination regarding injury to the domestic industry.

A separate provision of the statute provides that merchandise altered in form or appearance in minor respects should be considered part of the original order. The difference in treatment between minor alterations and later-developed merchandise is significant. Because the latter is included in the original order, the statute does not require a separate administrative proceeding before antidumping duties may be imposed. Where the line is drawn between the two categories is not clear.

The Injury Investigation

Like the Commerce Department investigation, the ITC's injury investigation has two phases. But whereas the Commerce preliminary phase is longer and more intensive, the reverse is true in the ITC's investigation. Consequently, rejection of a case at the preliminary phase of an ITC investigation is relatively uncommon. Also unlike a Commerce investigation, a negative preliminary determination terminates all activity in the case.

The Preliminary Investigation. The ITC must issue a preliminary determination within forty-five days of the initiation of an investigation. In this short period, the ITC collects available data regarding conditions in the domestic industry. It also compiles data on imports of the subject merchandise into the United States. When possible, the commission collects data covering the three full years before the initiation. The commission's staff usually holds an informal hearing at which interested parties present legal and factual arguments.

Under the statute, the ITC must render an affirmative determination, and the commission and Commerce must continue with their final and preliminary investigations, respectively, if the information available provides a reasonable indication that a domestic industry is injured by reason of the subject imports.[6] Under the prevailing standard, the ITC renders an affirmative determination unless (1) the record as a whole contains clear and convincing evidence of no material injury by reason of the subject imports and (2) no likelihood exists that contrary evidence will appear in a final investigation.

If the ITC does render a negative determination, the entire dumping investigation is terminated both at the ITC and at Commerce. The decision is subject to review at that point by the Court of International Trade. An affirmative determination is not appealable to the courts.

The Final Investigation. The ITC's final investigation includes the submission of detailed questionnaires to firms that are part of the domestic industry seeking information on their products, manufacturing processes, sales and revenue, financial condition, and other matters relating to the condition of the domestic industry. The ITC has the authority to issue an administrative subpoena if a firm fails to respond to a questionnaire and to seek judicial enforcement of that subpoena. The ITC staff conducts on-site verification of selected questionnaire responses and collects relevant information available from nonindustry sources such as trade publications and other government agencies.

The staff assigned to an investigation prepares a report for the ITC commissioners summarizing the results of the investigation. The parties usually submit briefs at this point as well. A few weeks before the commission's determination is due, the ITC holds a hearing at which the parties make presentations, the commissioners and staff question witnesses (usually officials of the firms participating in the investigation on each side of the issue), and the parties have a limited opportunity to question each other. Following the submission of posthearing briefs and the preparation of a final staff report to the commissioners, the commissioners vote at an open meeting. A summary of the commission's formal determination is published in the *Federal Register*, but the commissioners' opinions are published, along with the final staff report, in a separate publication. By statute, a tie vote of the commissioners favors the domestic industry.

The Domestic Industry. Before the ITC decides whether an industry is injured by reason of the subject imports, it must define the industry. Often these decisions are critical. Just as the Commerce Department's specification of the class or kind of imported merchandise defines the scope of its investigation, the ITC's definition of the industry determines the scope of its investigation.

The statute defines the domestic industry as "the producers as a whole of a domestic like product, or those producers whose collective output of a domestic like product constitutes a major proportion of the total domestic production of the product." The domestic-like product is "a product which is like, or in the absence of like, most similar in characteristics and uses with" the imports that are the subject of the investigation. In other words, the objective is to identify those domestic firms that manufacture the products most similar to, and therefore most likely to be affected by, the imports.

The ITC starts by looking at the Commerce Department's description of the class or kind of merchandise. Usually the issue is whether the class or kind description encompasses more than one like product. Sometimes the class or kind description includes a product and its component parts or a significant raw material involved in its production (such as hot-rolled and cold-rolled steel products) that were treated as separate like products, not raw material and finished goods. In other cases, the class or kind description, by its terms or in effect, includes different categories of products (such as the paper clips discussed earlier in this chapter).

The ITC looks at a variety of factors to determine whether to divide the class or kind of merchandise into one or more like products. The ITC considers the existence of separate markets for the products, the use of the same production facilities, the difference in price or value of the two products, and consumer perceptions and uses, that is, all the factors that tend to show whether the products are actually separate items of commerce.

If the ITC finds two or more like products, it defines two or more corresponding domestic industries. The ITC examines each industry separately. In such cases, it is not unusual for the ITC to reach a mixed determination: finding in the affirmative about one industry and in the negative about another. A dumping duty is imposed only on those imports covered by the ITC's affirmative determination.

Even after it defines the like products, the ITC can narrow the domestic industry on two grounds. First, if domestic producers in a region of the country sell a like product within that region and if demand for the like product in that region is not supplied from outside that region to a significant degree, the ITC may consider whether that regional industry is injured. If the subject imports are also concentrated in that region, then the ITC may consider whether the regional industry, defined as the producers in that region, has been injured.

Second, the ITC may consider whether firms that are related to foreign exporters or U.S. importers should be included within the domestic industry. Under current law, parties are related if one exercises direct or indirect control over another party. The principle behind this rule is that firms so related may be shielded by the effects of the imports and that inclusion of the firms in the assessment may distort the ITC's analysis. Generally, in deciding whether to include related parties, the ITC considers (1) the portion of domestic production attributable to a related party; (2) the reason for the importation (that is, whether the firm purchases the imports to continue domestic production and remain competitive or to benefit from lower cost purchases); and (3) whether the exclusion of the related party would skew the data for the rest of the industry. In most cases, the ITC includes the related party within the domestic industry.

Identifying the Relevant Imports. The ITC's role is to determine whether a domestic industry is injured "by reason of" the imports identified in the petition. After defining the domestic industry, therefore, the ITC must decide which imports to be considered. The inquiry begins with the imports that are the subject of the investigation. Imports that are not subject to the investigation—either because they are not within the class or kind of merchandise or are not from a country named in the petition—may not be considered a factor relevant to the condition of the domestic industry in the ITC determination, and may not be included in the dumping order. This has important implications for the utility of the dumping laws. As observers of tariffs have long recognized, tariffs targeted to certain countries or covering only narrow product lines are not complete measures of protection; imports of related products or identical products from other countries can also benefit from the reduction of competition in the U.S. market that results from such a focused tariff. The effect of the antidumping order therefore varies. The extent to which it provides a blanket of protection for an industry or establishes a focused countermeasure to particular trading practices depends on circumstances and the petitioner's petition.

The ITC is required to consider the subject imports from the countries specified in the petition cumulatively if (as they usually do) all imports under investigation compete with each other and with the domestic-like product. Theoretically, imports from a single country may not have an injurious effect by themselves, whereas the combined effects of dumped products from several countries might. In practice, however, this convention has led to situations in which imports from smaller, less developed countries were cumulated with large volumes of imports from trading powerhouses in Europe and Asia.

In 1988, Congress amended the statute to exclude negligible imports that have no discernible impact on the domestic industry. The commission grappled with the job of defining "negligible" for seven years. Efforts to quantify negligibility met with congressional insistence on determination on a case-by-case basis. In the 1994 amendments to the statute, however, Congress established a numerical standard: the commission must exclude imports from a country that constitute less than 3 percent of the total imports, so long as the total of all negligible imports is no greater than 7 percent of total imports. Interestingly, the commission's practice had been to consider negligibility from the perspective of U.S. consumption. The ITC had used a figure of about 1 percent in many cases. The 3 percent figure based on imports rather than on consumption might therefore have the effect of lowering the negligibility threshold in investigations in which total imports account for only a minor portion of total U.S. consumption.

The statute also makes exceptions for imports subject to an investigation that has been terminated, imports for which Commerce has made a negative preliminary determination (unless Commerce makes an affirmative final determination before the commission's final determination), and imports from Israel. The first two exceptions are housekeeping measures intended to resolve the question, raised in previous cases, of when an import is subject to investigation and therefore subject to cumulation. The third exception reflects Israel's trade and general political relations with the United States; imports from Israel are always entitled to a separate injury analysis without cumulation. The same exception applies to imports from Caribbean Basin Initiative countries.

The Injury Determination. The ITC injury analysis has generated the most controversy in international trade regulation. To a certain extent, the wrangling stems from a difference in the interpretation of the statutory text. The underlying dispute, however, emanates from the differences in the views of the ITC commissioners regarding the purpose of the statute itself.

The statute requires that the ITC render an affirmative determination if it concludes that the domestic industry is "materially injured *by reason of*" the subject imports (emphasis added). The law directs the commission to consider the volume of imports, the effects of imports on domestic prices for the like product, and the total impact of the imports on the domestic industry. The statute also provides an extensive list of commercial factors that the commission may consider and an admonition that the commission may evaluate any other factor it deemed relevant to the question of general injury. The act provides no guidance on the methodology or framework with which to perform the analysis.

While commissioners have used various methods for assessing injury over the years, two approaches prevail today. The first is known as the bifurcated analysis. The second is called unitary, or but-for, analysis.

The bifurcated approach begins by looking at the condition of the industry. Has the industry as a whole generated profits or losses? Has employment in the industry declined? Has production risen or declined during the three years for which the commission has collected data? If the trends in the industry are favorable, then the analysis stops. A negative determination results—the industry has not been injured. If the trends are unfavorable, the second stage of the bifurcated analysis comes into play.

The second step entails a form of causation analysis. In short form, this involves (1) a temporal correlation of import volumes with the industry's economic performance and (2) an analysis of data regarding nominal prices of actual transactions involving the domestic-like product and the imports to determine whether the imports undersell the domestic product in an absolute sense. If the amalgam of factors indicates that the imports have had an economic impact on the domestic industry, then the commissioners who use this methodology reach an affirmative determination.

The but-for approach starts from a different statutory premise. It rests on the proposition that the key statutory phrase—"by reason of"—requires a formalistic causation analysis that correlates imports with the industry's performance. The commissioners who use this methodology ask what the condition of the domestic industry would be absent the subject imports, regardless of its financial condition at the time of the petition. These officials are more likely to use economic concepts in their analysis. They put the statutory factors in an economic framework designed to measure directly the impact of imports on the domestic industry. The commissioners assess the degree to which the imports and the domestic-like products are substitutable. They ask whether domestic demand is elastic—that is, whether in the absence of dumped imports, domestic consumers would purchase an equivalent volume of domestic product. They evaluate the extent to which nonsubject imports would replace subject imports in the face of an antidumping order. Using available dumping margins from the Commerce investigation, these officials assess whether the difference in the "dumped" price and the price at a fair level under the statute would result in a material improvement in the domestic industry's fortunes. If the analysis shows that the imports have a material impact on the domestic industry, then these commissioners reach an affirmative determination.

While commissioners do not provide their theories or views on the trade laws in their opinions, one aspect of these analyses provides a key to the different perspectives that underlie the analyses. Any industry that has grown during the period of investigation but could be growing faster in the absence of dumped imports is much more likely to secure an affirmative determination under the but-for approach than under the trends approach. The commissioners who adopt the trends approach are more likely to view the dumping laws as a measure for protecting domestic industries. Advocates of the but-for approach would likely view the dumping laws as a measure designed to counter the effects of an outlawed commercial practice with as little distortion to the domestic markets as possible.

As discussed above, the courts have identified each element within the statute. They have sanctioned both the current approaches to the injury issue. The matter has been left to the discretion of individual commissioners. As a consequence, the selection of commissions to this bipartisan agency and the views of individual commissioners have at times generated enormous political controversy.

Recently, an opinion by the U.S. Court of Appeals for the Federal Circuit supported the unitary approach of injury analysis in unfair trade cases. In *Gerald Metals Inc. v. United States*,[7] the court determined that demonstrating that economic harm to the domestic industry occurred when imports of less than fair value are also in the market is not enough to show that imports were the cause of material injury. The court recognized that an affirmative injury determination requires both (1) present material injury and (2) finding that material injury is "by reason of" subject imports. "The antidumping statute mandates a showing of causal—not merely temporal—connection between the LTFV goods and the material injury." The appeals court held that the act "requires adequate evidence to show that the harm occurred by reason of the LTFV imports, not by reason of a minimal harm caused by LTFV goods."[8]

Threat and Material Retardation. Cases in which petitioners assert that a domestic industry is threatened with material injury or that the establishment of a domestic industry is materially retarded by reason of dumped imports raise difficult issues. By definition, these are cases in which the impact of the imports is not identifiable from historical market data or even from a straightforward economic analysis of current market conditions. In each case, the commission is asked to engage in a certain measure of speculation regarding circumstances not readily on the record of the proceeding.

In cases of a threat, the statute requires the ITC to consider a list of factors to determine whether the industry at issue faces material injury in the future. The factors include the capacity of the foreign industry to generate more imports, the historical trends in market penetration of imports, the effects of imports on U.S. prices, inventories of the subject merchandise in the U.S. market, the extent to which foreign producers can shift production facilities from other products to the subject imports, the impact of the imports on development and production efforts of the domestic industry, and any other adverse indications that the domestic industry is threatened with material injury because of the subject imports. The statute requires that the threat be imminent and that the determination not be based on conjecture or supposition.

The statutory scheme generates a real temptation to use the threat provisions to reach an affirmative determination in a close injury case, that is, a case in which the record almost supports an affirmative injury determination. Some critics have suggested that a number of commission threat determinations follow this approach.

The general view, however, is that the statutory proscription on supposition and conjecture requires more than a close injury case. Once the determination is made that the domestic industry is susceptible to injury, the commission must then point to some affirmative evidence that historic trends are likely to continue. This standard is obviously more difficult to establish, but, its defenders say, it is truer to the statutory spirit.

One of the simpler issues for the ITC involves claims that dumped imports materially retard the development of a domestic industry. The issue is simple, however, only because it arises so seldom. Participants in industries whose operations are not yet developed are not likely to invest time and money in pursuit of a dumping case. Moreover, timing is critical, as the actual development of an industry could turn the case from a material retardation case into an injury case. The rare cases that have been successful have typically involved long-term development or production efforts and where the petitioner could show substantial effort and commitment to establishing an industry, even though it had not yet begun production. Moreover, most successful cases concerned the development of a new product by existing firms; cases of entrepreneurial activity (such as a 1990 case involving flat-panel computer displays) are less likely to raise successful claims of material retardation.

Notably, the provision regarding material retardation is one of few U.S. trade laws that make an accommodation for what might be called infant industries, the type of industry that Alexander Hamilton identified in 1789 and formed the basis for U.S. tariff policy for the century that followed. Perhaps that fact highlights more than any other the dramatic extent to which U.S. international trade policy has changed over the past fifty years.

Suspension and Revocation

The Commerce Department or the ITC may terminate an investigation in certain circumstances without issuing a determination. The statute also provides procedures by which the department or the ITC may revoke an outstanding antidumping order. The standards are high, however, and, for all practical purposes, any effort by respondents to avoid the consequences of a continuing investigation or outstanding order are unlikely to be successful without the active support of the petitioning industry. Only if the respondent has altered its U.S. prices or eliminated its dumping margin for a substantial period will the department revoke an order.

Suspension and Withdrawal. Commerce may suspend an antidumping investigation if the exporters who account for "substantially all" (typically over 85 percent) of the subject imports agree

(1) to cease exports to the United States for 180 days, (2) to revise their prices to eliminate any dumping margin, or (3) to eliminate "the injurious effects" of the dumping. The suspension must be requested at least forty-five days before the Commerce Department is scheduled to issue its final determination. The petitioner must be given an opportunity to comment on the proposed revocation, although, in theory, the department may proceed with a suspension over a petitioner's objections.

The statute specifies that an agreement to eliminate the injurious effects of dumping (the third option above) must include an agreement that the imports will not undercut or suppress U.S. price levels and that the dumping margin will be reduced to 15 percent of U.S. levels during the period of investigation. To that end, the parties may ask the Commerce Department and the ITC to complete a suspended investigation. Not only will the department's investigation set a baseline dumping margin, but if both agencies reach negative determinations, the suspension agreement and the case are terminated.

The statutory provisions regarding the second option for a suspension agreement—the complete elimination of dumping—do not specify that the price of future exports not undercut or suppress U.S. prices. Thus, an exporter to the U.S. could, in theory, eliminate the margin by lowering prices in its home market while continuing to sell at prices above costs rather than by lowering prices or volumes in the U.S. market. In that event, the suspension agreement would be of no benefit to the domestic industry (and the Commerce Department would thus be unlikely to agree to such an arrangement).

The petitioner may withdraw its petition any time, subject to a Commerce Department determination of whether withdrawal would be in the public interest. Serious antitrust questions arise if the petitioner and respondents enter into a private arrangement regarding the price or volume of exports to the U.S. market. Typically, as in cases involving semiconductors and uranium, such arrangements have been made on a government-to-government basis, with the petitioner withdrawing the petition pursuant to that arrangement.

If the Commerce Department determines that a party is violating a suspension agreement, the department may immediately resume the investigation and suspend liquidation of entries of the subject merchandise. The agency took similar steps in a subsidy case involving Canadian softwood lumber; it terminated a government-to-government agreement and reinstated the investigation.

Revocation and Changed Circumstances. In the ordinary course of events, an antidumping order lives forever. Several outstanding orders are over twenty years old. As discussed, new orders will be subject to a "sunset review" on their fifth anniversary. But the sunset reviews will be conducted under standards similar to those already in place for revocation of an order. The impact of the new law is therefore difficult to predict.

The statute and Commerce Department regulations provide two grounds for revocation. The first is a finding that an exporter has not engaged in less-than-fair-value sales. Revocation on this ground must be supported by a Commerce Department finding of no dumping for each of the three years. The department therefore will not revoke an order unless the party entitled to revocation has participated in three consecutive reviews, and the revocation does not go into effect until those reviews are completed. This often does not occur until long after the three years have expired.

A party may also petition the department or the ITC for revocation of an order based on "changed circumstances." The party seeking revocation must make a preliminary showing to justify initiation of an investigation—in itself a high hurdle. Ordinarily, the department will revoke an order only on the basis of no dumped sales (discussed above) or a lack of interest by the domestic industry in maintaining the order.

The ITC's practice in a changed circumstances review is to assume that dumped imports will continue; otherwise, the argument runs, the review would fall within the Commerce Department's province. Essentially ignoring the level of imports, therefore, the commission looks to the state of the domestic industry to determine whether revocation of the order would result in material injury. Because the changed circumstances petition in many cases cites industry conditions linked closely to changes in import patterns stemming from the antidumping order itself, the commission frequently rejects petitions without instituting a formal investigation.

4
Countervailing Duties

One major area of trade disputes and litigation involves subsidies. Under international law, a *subsidy* is defined as a "financial contribution" provided by a government or other public body that confers a benefit. Examples of subsidies are government grants or loans to a company, tax relief, or any goods or services provided to industry by a government. This latter description of subsidies does not include government contribution to infrastructure, such as roads and airports.

Because of subsidies, global markets are distorted. The government subsidy generally either lowers the cost of production or increases the revenues of the subsidized producer. Competitors are then concerned that subsidized goods may be sold at lower prices than they would absent the subsidy. By injecting government capital into private transactions, global competitors argue that they are unfairly forced to compete with governments as well as other firms.

When subsidized goods move across borders, consumers benefit from the lower-priced autos or aluminum. Domestic producers of these goods, however, challenge this practice. The domestic industry demands that the subsidized imports be offset or countervailed. In the *countervailing* process governments apply additional customs duties to the cost of the subsidized imports. These duties are imposed by the importing state to eliminate any advantage of the subsidy and promote fairly traded competition.

The nature of subsidies is limited only by the purse and imagination of a particular government. Nearly every country engages in some form of subsidization of its domestic industries. The United States, for example, subsidizes research by the computer industry as well as agricultural exports. Despite these practices, the Organization for Economic Cooperation and Development determined that the United States offered fewer industrial subsidies than other developed states. Not surprisingly, the United States has also led a campaign to reduce the role of subsidies either unilaterally or multilaterally. The unilateral efforts to combat subsidies have led to U.S. uses of countervailing duty laws.

Multilateral efforts aimed at reducing subsidies go back to the Tokyo Round of the GATT and the Uruguay Round. At the conclusion of the Tokyo Round of the GATT in 1979, members had the option of joining the code on subsidies. Under this code, subsidies were identified and plans for addressing them were adopted. This particular step was not a smashing success as only a handful of GATT signatories agreed to adopt the code.

One major distinction about subsidies is whether they are export subsidies or domestic subsidies. Export subsidies are directly tied toward exports or export performance. Countries award export subsidies to producers to improve balance of payments, obtain hard currency, gain toeholds in particular markets, or achieve other goals. Export subsidies may come in the form of tax rebates tied to exports or low-cost government loans for export activities. The key point is that the receipt and the amount of the subsidy must be directly or indirectly tied to exports. Export subsidies are always prohibited and actionable and may be referred to in the United States as red-light subsidies. Other subsidies prohibited under the WTO are subsidies that are available only when a producer uses a certain degree of domestic content.

Domestic subsidies may be any other type of government financial assistance made available to producers. These subsidies may be classified as either direct or indirect. A direct subsidy may come in the form of cash grants, below–market rate loans, or tax credits.

Government upstream subsidies may also be subject to countervailing duty under U.S. law. Upstream subsidies are non-export-targeted subsidies granted to an input product used in the production of goods subject to a countervailing duty investigation. A government grant to a domestic steel industry, for example, may lower the cost of production of steel. If a domestic auto manufacturer were to purchase this cheaper steel, it would receive the indirect, upstream benefit of the subsidy. A government could decide to subsidize energy production costs by its public utilities. A producer of a high–energy consumption product, such as aluminum, would be said to benefit from this indirect upstream subsidy by using this subsidized energy

In some cases, a government may subsidize producers of raw agricultural products. When these goods are processed and later exported, the subsidy to the raw producer may be countervailable if

(1) demand for the raw product substantially depends on the demand for the processed product and (2) only limited value is added to the raw product by processing.

Unlike export subsidies, domestic subsidies may have a variety of goals, such as improving domestic technology, boosting employment, or promoting regional development or environmental quality. The WTO recognizes these goals. These green-light subsidies may, in some cases, be nonactionable. Subsidies for research and development are nonactionable as long as they are limited to "not more than 75 percent of the costs of industrial research or 50 percent of the costs of precompetitive development activity."

Similarly, subsidies granted to disadvantaged regions within the territory of a WTO member may be nonactionable. These subsidies must be part of a general plan of regional development and nonspecific. The subsidized regions must be previously identified as disadvantaged, based on neutral and objective criteria. The criteria must demonstrate that regional difficulties are not merely part of temporary circumstances. Under the WTO, for a country to qualify as a disadvantaged region, per capita or household income per capita, or gross domestic product per capita, must be below 85 percent of the average, and unemployment must be at least 110 percent of the average for the region. So, for example, a U.S. federal grant or offer of tax relief to stimulate growth in Appalachia may be nonactionable as long as the criteria are met. A grant to Michigan to help auto makers suffering from a bad quarter, however, would most likely be actionable.

A final type of nonactionable subsidy is related to environmental compliance. Under the WTO agreement on subsidies and countervailing measures, subsidies "to promote adaptation of existing facilities to new environmental requirements imposed by law and/or regulations" are nonactionable. These subsidies, however, must be limited to a one-time nonrecurring measure. The subsidy must not exceed 20 percent of the cost of adaptation. This subsidy cannot cover the cost of replacing and operating the assisted investment, which must be fully borne by firms, and must be available to all firms that can adopt the new measures.

Other subsidies are permissible but nonetheless actionable if they injure another WTO member. Serious prejudice to the domestic industry of the importing country is presumed to exist if the subsidy is over 5 percent of the value of the exported good, the subsidy is designed to cover operating losses of an industry, the subsidy covers more than a one-time operating loss by a specific exporter, and there is government forgiveness of debt or grants are made to repay debts.

U.S. countervailing duty law applies when the Department of Commerce determines that the government of a country or any public entity within the territory of a country is providing, directly or indirectly, a countervailable subsidy for the manufacture, production, or export of a class or kind of merchandise imported, or sold (or likely to be sold) for importation, into the United States. If the product is merchandise imported from a WTO member country, the International Trade Commission must determine that

(A) an industry in the United States—
    (i) is materially injured, or
    (ii) is threatened with material injury, or
(B) the establishment of an industry in the United States is materially retarded, by reason of imports of that merchandise or by reason of sales (or the likelihood of sales) of that merchandise for importation. In these situations, the International Trade Commission shall impose a countervailing duty on the imported goods. The amount of the countervailing duty shall be equal to the amount of the net countervailable subsidy.

Imported goods need not be sold to be subject to countervailing duty law. Leasing arrangements that are equivalent to sales will also be subject to countervailing duties. In investigations concerning leased goods, the Department of Commerce will examine (1) the terms of the lease, (2) commercial practice within the industry, (3) the circumstances of the transaction, (4) whether the leased product is integrated into the operations of the company, (5) the likelihood that the lease would be continued or renewed for a significant period, and (6) other relevant factors, such as whether the lease would permit the avoidance of antidumping or countervailing duties.

U.S. countervailing duty law also takes into account subsidies by international consortia. In the 1988 Omnibus Trade and Competitiveness Act, Congress specifically recognized the problems of subsidies supporting Airbus Industries. Airbus is a European international aircraft manufacturer. Several countries contribute subsidies to various parts of the aircraft constructed within their borders. Legislators were concerned that Airbus represented "a new and sophisticated tactic" to circumvent countervailing duty law. Congress wanted to ensure that all subsidies involved in the production of the final product were subject to countervailing duty law. Otherwise, only direct subsidies to the consortium may be countervailable. In determining the subsidy rate in a case involving such international consortia, the Department of Commerce cumulates subsidies directly granted to an international consortium as well as any subsidies received by consortium members in the production of the aircraft.

Procedures

Under U.S. law, private parties may simultaneously petition the Department of Commerce and the International Trade Commission for relief from injury due to subsidized goods. The Department of Commerce determines if a particular import is being subsidized and the degree of the subsidy. The International Trade Commission determines whether a domestic industry is injured by imports of a subsidized product. In some cases, the ITC may institute a countervailing duty investigation on its own motion. If the imports are not from members of the World Trade Organization, the only investigation needed is that of the Department of Commerce. Only goods from WTO member states are entitled to the injury determination.

The Department of Commerce examines several factors in determining whether a particular subsidy is actionable under U.S. law. One test is whether the subsidy is sector-specific. If the government of Panama decided to give investment tax credits to all Panamanian corporations, for example, this would be considered a generally available subsidy and not sector-specific. If the government granted a 20 percent tax rebate to the Panamanian steel industry, however, this subsidy would be specific to the steel industry and would be subject to U.S. countervailing duty laws.

Assume that a government charges a lower price on a natural resource, such as oil, to domestic firms than it charges importers. Because of the availability of oil at below–world market prices, the domestic producer is receiving a subsidy. If, however, this subsidy is made generally available to producers and it is used by a wide variety of industries, it is not sector-specific and not countervailable. If, conversely, the subsidy is provided only to energy-intensive industries, the subsidy may be countervailable. This benefit is not sector-specific; the Department of Commerce has determined that this is not an actionable subsidy.

In many cases, there may be a combination of actionable and nonactionable subsidies. In the case of grain-oriented silicon electrical steel, for example, the petitioner alleged that twenty-six subsidy programs were benefiting the Italian steel producer. The alleged subsidies included (1) government equity infusions provided to the exporter and predecessor companies of ILVA; (2) government debt forgiveness in connection with a restructuring plan; (3) debt forgiveness in connection with the transfer of Terni's assets to ILVA; (4) government loan guarantees; (5) preferential financing in the form of loans from the Ministry of Industry, Istituto per la Ricostruzione Industriale (IRI) bond issue loan, interest contributions, and capital grants; (6) personnel retraining grants, reductions in value-added tax, and interest grants for "indirect debts"; (7) urban redevelopment packages; (8) social security exemptions; (9) interest subsidies; (10) interest contributions; (11) insider financing; (12) subsidized Istituto Mobiliare Italiano (IMI) export financing; (13) national research plan for the iron and steel industry grant; (14) early retirement funding; (15) exchange risk guarantee program; (16) exemptions from local income taxes (ILOR) and profit taxes (IRPEG); (17) European Coal and Steel Community (ECSC) Article 54 loans; (18) European Social Fund grants; and (19) ECSC redeployment aid, Article 56(2)(b). In this investigation, all programs except numbers 7 (regional development) and 13 (funding research and development) may have been actionable subsidies.

In some investigations, the Department of Commerce does not include alleged subsidy programs. In these cases, the petitioner fails to provide evidence, information, or specific allegations. Often the petitioner has to rely on information from the exporting country to establish the existence of a subsidy. Government promotional materials, touting the benefits of investing in a particular state, are a useful starting point in marshaling evidence of subsidies. These materials often detail the nature and amounts of subsidies available to local producers. In some cases, petitioners have posed as corporations interested in investing in the state under investigation to gain this information from a foreign embassy.

Subsidies may be found to be *de minimis* in some cases. Under current U.S. law, a subsidy of 1 percent or less of the value of the imported goods is considered *de minimis*. If the subsidized goods are from a developing country, a subsidy of 2 percent or less will be considered *de minimis*. If a developing country notifies the Office of the U.S. Trade Representative that it has eliminated its export subsidy programs on an expedited basis, previously bestowed subsidies are considered *de minimis* if they are less than 3 percent.

U.S. courts have held that countervailing duty laws do not apply to exports from nonmarket economies. An export bonus granted by the Chinese government to a Chinese company exporting widgets, for example, is not countervailable. The Court of Appeals for the Federal Circuit has determined that because a nonmarket economy may set prices at any price, export or other subsidies do not further distort trade. Such imports, however, may be subject to antidumping duties.

Determining the Rate. After a final determination that subsidized imports are causing material injury to a domestic industry, the government establishes a countervailable subsidy rate. For each exporter and producer individually investigated, an estimated individual countervailable subsidy rate is imposed. Exporters and individuals not investigated individually face an estimated all-others rate. In certain cases, a single estimated countrywide subsidy rate, applicable to all exporters and producers, is imposed.

After a final determination, the International Trade Commission orders the posting of a cash deposit, bond, or other security for each entry of the subject merchandise in an amount based on the applicable estimated subsidy rate. The all-others rate is equal to the weighted average countervailable subsidy rates established for exporters and producers individually investigated. For purposes of this calculation, *de minimis* subsidies are excluded. In situations where the countervailable subsidy rates for all exporters and producers individually investigated are *de minimis,* the Department of Commerce may use any reasonable method to establish an all-others rate.

In some cases, Commerce may use a single countrywide subsidy rate for all exporters and producers from a particular state. This subsidy rate is determined by examining industrywide data regarding the use of subsidies determined to be countervailable.

Like antidumping cases, countervailing duty proceedings at the International Trade Commission are investigative, not adjudicatory, in nature. As in antidumping investigations, the staff at the International Trade Commission sends questionnaires to the domestic industry. These questionnaires are designed to determine the degree to which products compete. Also, the agency is trying to get an idea of the domestic industry condition.

One of the most important determinations under countervailing duty law as well as antidumping law is what products are subject to the investigation. Pursuant to section 771(4) of the Tariff Act of 1930, *industry* is defined as the "domestic producer as a whole of a like product or those producers whose collective output of the product constitutes a portion of the total domestic production of the product."

Like product is defined as "a product which is like, or in the absence of like, most similar in characteristics and uses with the article subject to the investigation." In other words, a like product is one with "the same intrinsic qualities and essential characteristics and uses as the subject imports."

Respondents and importers have a vested interest in arguing that their products are not like the domestic product and therefore are not competing. In this arena, questions of quality are often raised. This may be the only place where any producer claims that its products are inferior to those of the domestic industry. In other cases, a foreign producer may claim that because the quality is much higher than that of the domestic industry, the two products cannot possibly be said to compete. In the case of porcelain on steel cookware, for example, the Spanish producers asserted that the superior quality of their products was unlike that of the domestic producers. They sought an ITC finding of no like product or, alternatively, a finding of separate like products consisting of higher- and lower-quality porcelain on steel cookware.

Cumulation

In some cases, producers from several countries may subsidize their exports of a particular good. The individual impact of the subsidized imports of any one of these countries may not materially injure a U.S. domestic industry. Collectively, however, the impact of these subsidized imports may be a cause of material injury. To assess the full impact of these imports, the International Trade Commission "shall cumulatively assess the volume and effect of imports from two or more countries of like products subject to investigation."

There are three requirements for cumulation. First, the imports must compete with other imported products and the domestic like product. Second, the imports must be "marketed within a reasonably coincidental period." Finally, they must be subject to the pending investigation. In deciding whether to cumulate imports, the International Trade Commission will consider (1) "the degree of fungibility between imports from different countries and between imports and the domestic like product"; (2) the presence of sales or offers to sell in the same geographical markets of imports from different countries and the domestic like product; (3) the existence of common or similar channels of distribution for imports from different countries and the domestic like product; and (4) the simultaneous presence of imports in the market.

No individual factor determines whether the commission decides to cumulate. The International Trade Commission may, in some instances, cross-cumulate the impact of dumped imports with subsidized imports. The Court of International Trade has held that where all the other cumulation criteria are present in an investigation, cross-cumulation is in fact mandatory.

The preliminary investigation does not require a hearing. At this level, parties may participate in a staff conference and testify and answer questions from the International Trade Commission staff. During the final investigation, hearings are held on request. As a matter of practice, parties generally request a hearing. The hearing is simply an opportunity for parties to put a gloss on the argument that they have made in their written submissions. Oral testimony is rarely, if ever, dispositive of an outcome. Written testimony and ex parte communication, as well as the commission's own investigations, are generally granted as much, if not more, weight than information gathered at hearings.

In a countervailing duty investigation, the respondent's best strategy is to demonstrate that there are no subsidies, subsidies are de minimis, or subsidies are nonactionable. Respondents face several obstacles. A primary obstacle is time. The petitioner has spent significant time and resources in preparing the petition with time on its side. The respondent must reply within thirty days of the petition. Second, the respondent in a countervailing duty case must obtain the cooperation of its government in a public airing of its subsidy practices in this short time frame. The International Trade Administration and the International Trade Commission will rely on the "best information available." If the respondent cannot respond quickly and in a readily verifiable manner, the agencies may ignore their responses. Instead, the agencies may rely on information supplied by a well-prepared petitioner.

Should an affirmative determination be reached by the International Trade Commission, a countervailing duty may be imposed on the subsidized imports.

Countervailing duty investigations may also be settled by diplomatic means. The WTO agreement envisions that members will notify the WTO before establishing a new subsidy program. Parties at the International Trade Commission may also settle their dispute by agreement. The result may be a quota or other restriction on imports. Countervailing duty cases may be brought before, simultaneously, or instead of antidumping investigations. In some cases, attorneys have used countervailing duty investigations to fish for evidence for antidumping cases. In cases dealing with exports from a non–WTO member state or from countries without WTO equivalent arrangements, such as Taiwan, the absence of a finding of injury makes countervailing duty investigations cheaper to institute than antidumping cases.

The petition is filed by a domestic industry. The Department of Commerce may terminate the investigation within twenty days if it finds no evidence of subsidy. If the department does not terminate the investigation at this time, the inquiry proceeds at the International Trade Commission. Within forty-five days of filing the petition, the ITC reaches either a negative preliminary determination, terminating the case, or an affirmative determination. An affirmative determination means that the commission has found a reasonable indication that a domestic industry is materially injured or threatened with material injury.

The Department of Commerce then continues its inquiry, investigating the nature and amount of the subsidy. Forty days after the affirmative preliminary determination by the International Trade Commission, the department issues either an affirmative or negative preliminary determination. Commerce may designate a case as "extraordinarily complicated"; in these cases, the agency may take 105 days to reach its preliminary determination. This additional time is also granted if the investigation involves allegations of upstream subsidies.

Seventy-five days after reaching its preliminary determination, the Department of Commerce announces its final determination. A negative final determination terminates the investigation. After an affirmative determination, however, the rate of the subsidy is transmitted to the International Trade Commission. Forty-five days after receipt of the information from the Department of Commerce, the commission must render its final determination.

Injury Analysis

The models of injury analysis for countervailing duty investigations are similar to those applied in antidumping cases. The standard of material injury under countervailing duty cases is "harm which is not inconsequential, immaterial or unimportant." By statute, the International Trade Commission must evaluate (1) the volume of imports of the merchandise under investigation, (2) the effect of these imports on prices in the United States for like products, and (3) the impact of these imports on domestic operations of domestic producers. This last provision is designed to guard against "false negative determinations" in investigations featuring a domestic industry composed of producers with healthy offshore operations and yet injured domestic operations. Inclusion of the foreign operations of the domestic producers would not accurately reflect the domestic industry condition.

No one factor is dispositive. As with antidumping investigations, the International Trade Commission cannot weigh causes of material injury. During an investigation, for example, the commission may find that the domestic industry suffers because of excessive debt loads, inefficiency, or the rise of other domestic products that compete with the product under investigation. If subsidized imports are still a contributing cause of the material injury, they may be countervailed.

In some cases, countervailing duties may be applied retroactively. This situation involves "critical circumstances." Such circumstances exist when an exporter, faced with the filing of a countervailing duty petition, rapidly increases exports in attempts to outrace the ITC determination. On petition by the domestic industry that critical circumstances exist, the International Trade Commission will assess (1) the likelihood that an import surge resulted from efforts to circumvent an order, (2) whether foreign economic conditions led to massive imports, and (3) whether the impact of the massive imports is likely to continue after issuance of the order.

Although the statute addresses factors to be considered in evaluating injury, the act provides no guide to the ITC in injury analysis. Several methods of assessing trade injury have developed. One method of analysis is the bifurcated method. Under this analysis, the ITC examines two questions. First, is the domestic industry suffering material injury? Second, are there subsidized imports? If the answer to each is in the affirmative, the decision maker typically votes in favor of a finding of material injury. This mode of analysis uses trend analysis and is flawed in its simplicity. Although the bifurcated method leads to a large number of affirmative findings, it fails to link subsidized goods with injury to the domestic industry.

The trend analysis also leads to false determinations. Assume that the domestic industry controls 75 percent of the market and is doing well by all objective analysis (sales, prices, wages, and employment are all improving). Now let us assume that the foreign producers that account for the remaining 25 percent of the market are selling subsidized goods and the rate of the subsidy is 20 percent.

Can we say that the subsidized imports are causing material injury to the domestic industry? Under a bifurcated analysis, the answer might well be no. Because the industry appears to be doing well, under this method of analysis it cannot be said to be incurring material injury. Thus, the question of whether the subsidized goods are the cause of this injury is not even reached.

The flaw of this analysis is obvious. Even though the domestic industry is doing well, it might be doing better. If the subsidized sales were not present, the market share of the domestic industry might be 85 percent or more. Wages, employment, and sales could be higher still. Thus, subsidized sales may be a cause of material injury to even a healthy industry.

More commonly, the bifurcated approach results in false positives. Assume, for example, that the domestic industry is losing market share and prices are depressed. Also assume that foreign manufacturers, selling a superior product, use superior technology, take advantage of larger economies of scale, and even provide lower cost financing. Also suppose that the foreign manufacturer is selling these goods subsidized at a rate of 10 percent. A decision maker using the bifurcated method would probably ignore any considerations other than the facts that the domestic industry is unhealthy and there is a subsidy and would find in the affirmative.

Another method of analysis employed at the ITC is the unitary analysis. With this method of analysis, the commissioner assesses whether the domestic industry is incurring domestic injury by reason of subsidized imports. The injury must be linked directly to the subsidy. In analysis such as this, the ITC decision maker typically employs an economic model form of analysis. This model determines the Comparative Analysis of Domestic Industry Condition.[1] With a CADIC analysis, the decision maker must try to replicate the condition of the domestic industry to simulate a market free of subsidized goods. The CADIC approach is the method of analysis most consistent with the GATT.

CADIC analysis leads to consideration of other domestic sellers and fairly traded goods in the market when assessing damage.

Assume that the U.S. widget industry files a countervailing duty petition. Also assume that the U.S. widget manufacturers control 60 percent of the domestic market. Now assume that the remaining 40 percent of the market is controlled by foreign imports, some subsidized: 10 percent of the imported goods are subsidized goods from Burkina Faso, and the remaining 30 percent are fairly traded goods from Japan. If one pursues a CADIC approach to this injury analysis, he would remove the impact of the subsidized goods from the market. The 10 percent of subsidized sales from Burkina Faso might now go to the domestic industry. If this is the case, a decision maker might conclude that the domestic industry is suffering material injury by reason of the subsidized goods. In other words, if the subsidized goods were not in the market, the sales would have gone to the domestic industry or to the fairly traded goods.

But now take another approach. Assume the same facts as above regarding market share and rate of subsidy. But envision a state where the domestic industry is in horrible decline. The decline may be attributed to failure to modernize equipment because of massive debt burdens from leveraged buyouts or some other corporate mismanagement. At the same time, assume that the fairly traded imports are really coming on like gangbusters and are perceived by purchasers as a superior product.

Under a CADIC approach in this particular pattern of facts, there is no assurance that the domestic industry will prevail. The decision maker may conclude that if the subsidies were removed from the market, the sales would not necessarily flow to the domestic industry. The fairly traded imports might receive the benefit of the elimination of the subsidy. Accordingly, in such a case, there is no reason to impose countervailing duties. Imposition of countervailing duties might benefit only the fairly traded imports and not the domestic industry.

An even more curious situation is one in which all foreign imports are subsidized goods. One can have a situation where even if the subsidized goods are offset by countervailing duties, the subsidized goods are still preferred by the consumer. One must then inquire whether the domestic industry has been injured *by reason of the subsidized goods*. If not, the countervailing duties serve no purpose other than to increase costs to the consumer. The duties will not drive the consumer to purchase domestic goods. Unless the goods are truly fungible, the countervailing duties will not transfer the allegedly lost sales to the domestic industry.

5

The Escape Clause

In some cases, a U.S. domestic industry may be seriously injured by fairly traded, nondumped, or subsidized imports. Fairly traded imports may be on the rise because of the lowering or elimination of tariffs under negotiations at the World Trade Organization or from the development of the United States as a new market. Section 201 of the Trade Act of 1974,[1] commonly referred to as the escape clause, provides a mechanism for domestic industries to seek relief from foreign import competition. Relief under this section was originally designed to allow the domestic industry time to adjust to rising import competition, thus allowing them to escape from new lower tariff levels and competition.

Relief may come in the form of increased tariffs on imports, import quotas, or negotiations with foreign states. Because of the absence of any unfair action by the foreign exporter and the wider range of sanctions available, section 201 requires not only a finding of serious injury by the U.S. International Trade Commission but action by the president. Even if the ITC determines that an industry is seriously injured by increased quantities of foreign imports, the president can decline to grant the relief recommended by the ITC. Historically, the chief executive does not grant relief readily under section 201.

Procedures for Investigations

A section 201 investigation may be initiated by a petition to the International Trade Commission by an industry trade association, company, or certified or recognized union that represents an industry. An investigation may also be launched by a request by the president, the U.S. trade representative, or the House Ways and Means or Senate Finance Committee. The International Trade Commission may also institute a section 201 investigation on its own motion.

Petitions for section 201 relief must include a description of the goals of relief. These purposes include helping a firm move to the production of other goods and assisting in a firm's competitiveness.

Although the ITC can, in theory, conclude that a petition is deficient, it has never refused to initiate an investigation on a properly filed petition. There are limits on petitions for relief. After an industry receives relief, another section 201 investigation cannot be initiated for the length of time equal to the length of time of relief granted. If relief is granted for three years, for example, a subsequent investigation may not be initiated until three years after the termination of the original relief. Petitioners who failed to gain relief in an earlier section 201 investigation may not file another petition for one year.[2]

Pursuant to the statute, a domestic industry petition must address steps taken to facilitate a "positive adjustment to import competition." According to the House report about the legislation, these industry adjustment plans may include (1) an evaluation of current industry problems, (2) recommended actions for manufacturers and employees to increase their competitiveness, (3) recommended federal actions to improve domestic competitiveness or adjustment to imports, and (4) an analysis of the impact of import relief on these objectives.[3] Petitioners may consult with federal agencies in assessing the adjustment plans. These consultations must be approved by the USTR.[4]

Timing and Conduct of Investigations

The International Trade Commission promptly initiates a section 201 investigation. The commission makes an injury determination within four months. In "extraordinarily complicated" investigations, however, the injury determination may last as long as seventy days.[5]

If the ITC determines that a domestic industry is experiencing serious injury, the commission makes its remedy recommendation. This recommendation must be made within six months from the date on which a petition is filed. Only those commissioners who vote in the affirmative in the injury determination phase can offer remedy recommendations.

As with countervailing duty or antidumping petitions, the commission relies on the best information available. Data are obtained from questionnaires sent to the domestic industry, importers, and purchasers. This information is aggregated and used in the commission reports. Reports regarding individual firms are treated as confidential. Consumers may also submit information to the commission but seldom do so. Information is also obtained from the Department of Labor and other government agencies. Two to three months after the initiation of an investigation, a public hearing is held. The domestic industry, exporters, importers, and consumers may present evidence regarding injury and adjustment plans.[6]

Methodology

As under the unfair trade laws, the initial and crucial determination of the domestic industry must be made. *Domestic industry* is defined as the domestic producers of articles "like or directly competitive with" the imported merchandise under review. As part of its analysis of like products, the commission considers physical characteristics, prices, consumer perceptions, channels of distribution, and methods of production.

Products at different levels of development may be considered like products when an import at a different stage from the domestic product has the same economic effects on the domestic article as imports at the same level. In the investigation of apple juice, for example, the commission determined that the domestic industry was U.S. apple growers, concentrators, and retail processors.[7]

In some investigations, members of the domestic industry may also import the products under investigation as well as manufacture them domestically. When considering these firms, the ITC considers only the domestically produced goods as part of the domestic industry. In the investigation of heavyweight motorcycles, for example, the commission determined that domestic subsidiaries of Japanese motorcycle producers were part of the domestic industry. The Japanese subsidiaries used imported parts in over 50 percent of their domestic production.[8]

In some investigations, the domestic firms may produce several similar products. In these cases, they assert that there are several domestic industries. This tactic is particularly useful when the domestic producers manufacture some products that are suffering serious injury and others that are quite healthy. In the investigation of certain metal castings,[9] for example, the petitioners maintained that there were seven domestic industries. The commission ultimately determined that there were eleven domestic industries. In the investigation of certain knives,[10] arguments were made that the relevant domestic industries were outdoor knives, indoor knives, and Swiss army knives.

When evaluating a case under section 201, the petitioner must demonstrate that imports are increasing. Generally, imports are rising in either absolute or relative terms. In other words, imports may be increasing either in quantity or in percentage of domestic market share. It has been argued that the imports must be rising in absolute terms.

The legislative history of section 201 never defines serious injury. The legislative history does offer some guidance, noting that "as barriers to international trade are lowered, some industries and workers inevitably face serious injury, dislocation and perhaps economic extinction."[11] Arguably, a high standard such as extinction may be required for relief under section 201. Another definition of serious injury is "an important, crippling or mortal injury, one having permanent or lasting consequences." The standard for a "threat of serious injury" is one that is "real rather than speculative" and that such injury is "highly probable in the foreseeable future." [12]

As with investigations regarding countervailing duty, the statute does not specify the methodology to be used. The act does require the commission to consider (1) significant cutbacks in productive facilities, such as plant closings; (2) lack of profit for a substantial number of domestic firms; and (3) serious unemployment or underemployment.[13]

In evaluating the threat of serious injury, the commission considers such relevant economic factors as (1) declining sales or market share, a bloated inventory, and drops in production, profits, wages, or employment; (2) problems in capital financing for modernization or funding for research and development; and (3) dumping in the U.S. market because of limiting exports to third-country markets.[14]

The statute requires that increased imports be a "substantial cause" of serious injury, "not less than any other cause."[15] Unlike antidumping investigations, the commission may weigh causes when evaluating injury under section 201.

One form of analysis is referred to as the three-curve analysis. This method examines three components: (1) domestic demand, (2) domestic supply, and (3) import supply. In the investigation of wood shakes and shingles, ITC Vice Chairman Liebeler and Commissioner Brunsdale noted that the domestic demand for wood shakes and shingles may be influenced by consumer preferences, new housing activity, and prices of substitute products (such as asphalt shingles, clay tile, aluminum siding, and slate). The domestic supply depends on variables such as production technology and the availability of production inputs such as labor and red cedar logs. The import supply similarly depends on availability of red cedar logs and other inputs. Other variables including foreign demand also play a role in determining input supply.

The three factors of domestic demand, domestic supply, and import supply determine the domestic market price, the quantity sold by all domestic firms, and the total quantity of imports. Assume that the demand for shakes and shingles drops because of a slow-down in housing starts or a shift in builder preferences to tiles. This drop in demand adversely affects both domestic and foreign producers, as market prices decline for both. According to this model of analysis, "serious" injury experienced by the domestic producers is caused by the decline in domestic demand.

The domestic industry may also be injured by an adverse shift in the domestic supply. This shift may be attributed to higher production costs or declining productivity. Higher prices for the domestic product make the domestic product less competitive. The new domestic price attracts foreign competitors and additional imports.

Similarly, shifts in the foreign supply curve can also injure the domestic industry. An increase in foreign supply due to lower foreign costs of inputs, increased productivity, or decreased foreign demand may lead to a rise in imports. Cheaper foreign imports lower the domestic price and expand consumption. Although under these circumstances domestic consumption may increase, lower domestic prices injure domestic firms. Domestic shipments might drop. According to Liebeler and Brunsdale, increased imports would be a cause of injury to the domestic industry. They reason that "the causal factor that initiates the changes in the domestic market is the change in import supply."[16]

Another form of analysis used in section 201 investigations is shift-share analysis. This method examines only two possible causes of serious injury: decreased demand and increased imports. One major flaw is the failure to discriminate between increased imports and declining domestic productivity. Shift-share analysis does not adequately address issues of causality and may lead to false positive determinations. Legislative intent clearly denies relief in investigations where the rise in imports is attributable to escalating domestic production costs.

Another way to evaluate causation is to examine the trends in the domestic industry. If the domestic industry is suffering serious injury and imports are rising, causation is assumed.

Remedy Recommendations

After determining whether an industry is seriously injured or threatened with serious injury under section 201, the commission engages in the remedy phase of the investigation. The commissioners who voted in the affirmative on injury must recommend to the president the most effective remedy to assist "the efforts of the domestic industry to make a positive adjustment to import competition."[17] Unlike the procedure with countervailing duty or antidumping investigations, a tie vote does not mean victory for the petitioner. Should the commissioners' determinations result in a tie, each opinion goes to the president, who selects one as the opinion of the commission.

The ITC holds a separate public hearing during the remedy phase. The commission at this time must consider (1) actions to "prevent or remedy the injury or threat," (2) actions recommended by adjustment plans, (3) "any individual commitment submitted to the Commission," (4) competitiveness in domestic and world markets, and (5) the potential of international consultations to remedy the injury or facilitate adjustment.

Although commissioners who voted in the negative during the injury phase cannot vote on a remedy, they may offer separate views on a remedy to the president. The following remedies are available:

1. Tariff increases of not more than 50 percent ad valorem above the existing rate. A tariff of 20 percent ad valorem, for example, could be raised to no more than 70 percent ad valorem.

2. Tariff-rate quotas. Under a tariff-rate quota, the imports are subjected to a multiple-rate tariff depending on import penetration. A tariff on honey, for example, may allow the initial 1,000 tons to enter at a rate of 10 percent. The next 1,000 tons might enter at 20 percent, while the remaining honey might enter at 25 percent.

3. Quotas. Quotas imposed as section 201 relief must at least equal the amount or value imported during the most recent period that is "representative" for the imports under investigation. Quotas must be applied on a most-favored-nation basis and must not violate the international trade obligations of the United States. They

may be global or may be administered on a nation-by-nation basis, but the quota must be "administered equitably."[18]

4. Others. The International Trade Commission may recommend other appropriate adjustment measures such as suspension of privileges of the Generalized System of Preferences or of expedited trade adjustment assistance.

Any of the remedies discussed above may be combined. No remedy may exceed the amount necessary to correct the serious injury caused by the increased imports. The commission can also recommend that the president initiate international consultations to address the underlying cause of the increase in imports or otherwise alleviate the injury or threat or that he implement any other action authorized by law that is likely to facilitate positive adjustment to import competition.

In some instances during a section 201 investigation, the ITC may determine that the injury is caused by an unfair trade practice such as dumping or antitrust violations. The commission may refer this information to the appropriate federal agency.

As with the countervailing duty laws, petitioners in section 201 investigations may be eligible for provisional import relief on demonstrating that "critical circumstances" are present. To establish the existence of such circumstances, the domestic industry must demonstrate both "a substantial increase in imports (either actual or relative to domestic production) over a relatively short period of time" and that any delay in taking remedial measures "would cause harm that would significantly impair the effectiveness of such action."[19] Any petition for a finding of critical circumstances must be made at least thirty days before the commission issues its report to the president. If critical circumstances are found, the commission recommends to the president the form of provisional relief to be granted. The president has seven days to respond to this recommendation. Provisional relief may come in the form of increased tariffs, quotas, or immediate suspension of liquidation. These remedies may be combined. If the ITC reaches a negative determination or the president declines to grant final relief, provisional relief is terminated.

Case Studies

In 1984, the footwear industry sought relief under section 201. The ITC unanimously issued a negative injury determination. Although in its determination the ITC noted rising imports, domestic plant closing, and drops in domestic employment, the profitability of the remaining producers supported a negative determination.

Surprised and angered by the result, Congress amended section 201 as part of the Trade Act of 1984. The amended act directed the ITC to consider "the closing of plants or the underutilization of production capacity" as part of the injury analysis. The new act admonished the ITC not to base decisions solely on factors such as the profitability of the domestic producers. The act states that "the presence or absence of any factor which the Commission is required to evaluate . . . shall not necessarily be dispositive of whether an article is being imported into the United States in such increased quantities as to be a substantial cause of serious injury or threat of serious injury."

The Senate directed the ITC to revisit the nonrubber footwear investigation. Unsurprisingly, this investigation under the amended act resulted in a unanimous affirmative injury determination. The ITC recommended a quota on nonrubber footwear valued over $2.50 for a period of five years. President Reagan rejected this quota recommendation. He stated his belief that such import barriers would impose substantial costs on U.S. consumers. In addition, the president was concerned that quotas might spark retaliation from our trading partners and reduce U.S. exports. President Reagan concluded that the proposed relief would have only a short-term benefit for the domestic industry. He further observed that the domestic industry had become more competitive during recent years without quotas and had become more vulnerable to international competition while operating under quotas.

The domestic copper industry also unsuccessfully sought relief under section 201. Although the industry won an affirmative injury determination, the ITC was divided as to the remedy. While two commissioners preferred tariffs, and two recommended quotas, a fifth felt that no remedy should be granted. President Reagan declined to grant relief. He determined that relief was "not in the national economic interest." President Reagan observed that the copper-producing states, with copper as a leading export, were also debt-ridden. Thus, to stem the international debt crisis, increased trade barriers on copper would have more significant effects on the U.S. and world economy.

The president's refusal to grant relief in the copper investigation added to congressional dissatisfaction. The Textile and Apparel Trade Enforcement Act of 1985 included a section directing the president to negotiate voluntary agreements with copper-producing countries. This provision would roll back copper production to 1982 levels.[20] President Reagan vetoed this legislation.

The section 201 investigation of the heavyweight motorcycle industry is perhaps the classic example of how section 201 is to be applied. In 1982, Harley-Davidson was the only remaining domestic producer of heavyweight motorcycles. The ITC determined that increased imports were a substantial cause of serious injury to the domestic industry and issued an affirmative injury determination. In the remedy phase of the investigation, the ITC recommended the imposition of an additional incremental tariff for five years.

The president granted modified relief to the industry, replacing the ITC recommended tariff with a tariff rate quota to be applied for imports above the quota levels. President Reagan granted relief to Harley-Davidson because the firm had provided a viable plan to adjust to competition in a postrelief economy. The Harley-Davidson plan proved accurate. Inventory and quality controls, combined with a successful marketing plan, returned the motorcycle manufacturer to the road of competitiveness. In a unique display of confidence and stability, in 1987, Harley-Davidson requested that the relief be terminated a year before expiration. President Reagan granted this request.

The steel industry has been the most successful proponent of section 201. In 1983, the ITC reached an affirmative injury determination in a section 201 investigation concerning stainless steel and alloy tool steel. The investigation was initiated at the request of the USTR pursuant to section 301. President Reagan granted a mixture of relief. Increased tariffs were imposed on imports of stainless steel sheet, strip and plate, and flat-rolled steel. Quotas were imposed on imports of nonrolled stainless steel. The disparity in relief reflected the president's recognition that each sector of the industry faced different degrees of pressure in international competition. This combination of relief was granted for four years, as opposed to the three years of relief recommended by the ITC.[21] Orderly marketing agreements were then established between the United States and major steel exporting states.

The carbon steel industry also sought relief under section 201 during this period. In what was billed as "the Superbowl of trade litigation," Bethlehem Steel and the United Steelworkers of America petitioned the ITC to protect nine types of steel. A divided ITC reached an affirmative injury determination for steel ingots, blooms, billets, slabs, and sheet bars. These products represented some 70 percent of steel imports. The commission issued a negative determination regarding imports of steel wire rod, railway-type products, bars, and pipe and tube.

A combination of relief was recommended, including tariff rate quotas, market share quotas, and tariffs. One commissioner urged conditioning relief on salary cuts of 20 percent in the industry as part of an industry adjustment plan.

President Reagan rejected the ITC recommendations. He provided relief to the steel industry outside the section 201 process. Instead of tariff increases or quotas, the president instructed the USTR to negotiate voluntary restraint agreements (VRAs) with steel-exporting nations. Although President Reagan declined to follow the recommendations of ITC Vice Chairman Liebeler to tie relief to an industry adjustment plan, Congress adopted this concept. In the Steel Import Stabilization Act of 1984, Congress required industry relief to be conditioned on modernization of plant or reinvestment.

The WTO agreement on safeguards prohibits the use of voluntary restraint agreements. Member states are obliged to use escape-clause measures such as section 201 as a precursor to imposing comprehensive and temporary industry protection plans.

6

Problems of Imports from Nonmarket Economies

Section 406 of the Trade Act of 1974 gives the president the authority to impose protective quotas and tariffs when a domestic industry is threatened with market disruption by increasing imports from a Communist country. This statute is similar to section 201 (the escape clause) in that no allegations of unfair trade practices are required and relief requires presidential decision. The limit to imports from Communist countries and the absence of other relief are two notable differences.

The purpose of section 406 is to provide temporary relief to domestic producers when a rapidly rising increase in imports from Communist nations disrupts the market. Market disruption, as defined by section 406, exists "within a domestic industry whenever imports of an article, like or directly competitive with an article produced by such domestic industry, are increasing rapidly, either absolutely or relatively, so as to be a significant cause of material injury, or threat thereof, to such domestic industry."[1] The rationale behind this narrowly drafted act, targeted solely against Communist nations, envisions a situation where imports flood the domestic market outside the constraints of market forces. Since centrally planned, nonmarket economies set the price and amount produced of any given article, market share can be quickly built without regard to traditional market considerations. Domestic producers, lacking this ability, can be washed away in a sea of Communist imports flooding the market. Accordingly, section 406 affords them some protection.

Procedures

Section 406 action begins with the filing of a petition for import relief with the International Trade Commission. The ITC then investigates the alleged increase in Communist imports to see whether market disruption exists.

When making such an investigation, the commission searches for evidence of rapidly increasing imports from a Communist country that are a significant cause of material injury or threat of material injury to a domestic industry. The rapid rise of imports may be in either absolute or relative terms. Assume that the domestic market for a product is 1 million units. Assume that subject imports rise from 100,000 units to 150,000 when the domestic market is contracting to 800,000 units. This might constitute a rapid rise under section 406. The commission interprets *rapidly increasing* to mean "abnormal increases in imports."

The term *significant cause* has been interpreted by the commission as a lower standard than the substantial cause used in section 201 investigations. To qualify as a significant cause, imports must be "at least an important cause of material injury." The imports under investigation, however, need not be a greater or equivalent cause of material injury. The standard of material injury is similar to that employed in antidumping and countervailing duty investigations. Each of these elements must be present to support a determination of market disruption. If the commission reaches a positive determination, it will forward its findings to the president with recommendations for domestic industry relief. The president then determines what form of relief will be granted, or if any relief will be granted at all.

In its twenty-two-year history, only four section 406 investigations have culminated in positive determinations of market disruption. Of these four, the president authorized relief only once.

Honey Imports from China

In 1993, representatives from the domestic honey industry petitioned the International Trade Commission to investigate an increase in Chinese honey imports.[2] The ensuing investigation found a market disruption and recommended a schedule of tariff-rate quotas to the president.

From 1989 to 1992, Chinese honey imports rose by 141 percent while the domestic industry performed erratically. Domestic beekeepers' net income fell by 14 percent while honey packers' income rose by 8 percent. Unemployment and underemployment statistics reflected no significant problems. Thus, the industry was not experiencing material injury.

Conflicting indicators, however, suggested that the profitability of the industry was in decline. Domestic honey packers had faced mounting inventories since 1992. The domestic industry had lost 13 percent of the domestic market. Furthermore, domestic beekeepers fell under financial stress when trying to maintain and upgrade their equipment.

The ITC concluded that "the vulnerable state of the U.S. industry, as illustrated by its declining profitability and rising inventories, in addition to the potential for diversion of Chinese honey exports to the U.S. market, indicate that the U.S. honey industry is threatened with material injury." Three factors led to this conclusion: (1) beekeepers have few market options outside of producing and selling honey; (2) Chinese honey and domestic honey are close substitutes; and (3) the planned suspension of federal agricultural support programs would exacerbate the financial difficulties of domestic beekeepers.

Proposed Remedies

Chairman Newquist and Commissioners Rohr and Nuzum recommended a three-year tariff-rate quota: Imports of up to 12.5 million pounds of honey would face a 25 percent ad valorem tariff, and imports exceeding 12.5 million pounds would face a 50 percent ad valorem tariff. Under such relief, the commissioners predicted that the domestic industry would recapture part of its lost market share and see a 2 percent increase in price and 4 percent increase in quantity produced. They also recommended a review of the tariffs after three years, or earlier if the status of federal loan programs to honey producers changed.

Vice Chairman Watson perceived a lesser threat from Chinese honey and recommended minimal relief: a 15 percent ad valorem tariff on the first 60 million pounds of imported honey and a 25 percent tariff on imports exceeding 60 million pounds. Watson emphasized that the ITC's remedy should remain flexible to respond to any increase in demand for honey.

Commissioner Crawford recommended that a flat-rate tariff of 10 percent be applied to all Chinese honey; he warned that tariff-rate quotas would lead to unnecessarily high social costs. With tariff-rate quotas, Chinese officials would have to choose which exporters would be subject to the lower duty. The likely result would be a new Chinese administration dedicated to solving allocative problems. Moreover, U.S. officials would have to monitor the quantity of honey flowing in from China. Thus, needless administrative costs in China and monitoring costs in the United States would be incurred. A flat tariff, Crawford reasoned, would eliminate unnecessary social costs and would promote the market's ability to respond to increases in demand.

In dissenting from the four-member majority's finding of a market disruption, Commissioner Brunsdale focused on the health of the domestic honey industry. She acknowledged that Chinese honey imports increased drastically during the 1989–1992 period. But she also observed that domestic production increased by nearly 25 percent during this period.

Brunsdale distinguished the types of honey from different sources. Domestic honey packers had complained that the darker Chinese honey was often plagued by high moisture content, was mixed with sweeteners and chemical additives, and tasted sour because of fermentation. Consequently, Chinese honey in the United States had been used primarily for industrial purposes. The lighter, sweeter-tasting, retail-oriented domestic product found substitutes in honey from Argentina and Canada. The increase in domestic demand, however, had been generated largely by industrial users. Mexican honey was a comparable substitute and would likely take the place of Chinese imports if the latter were restricted. Other countries had much higher tariffs than the United States but still imported significant amounts of Chinese honey.

Brunsdale further observed that "the financial experience of beekeepers has been linked closely to U.S. government program payments." She noted that, in 1988, government subsidies accounted for 50 percent of a beekeeper's income. By 1992, this figure dropped to 13 percent. Given the decline in payments, the domestic industry was performing remarkably and was therefore not materially injured or threatened by material injury from an increase in Chinese imports.

Brunsdale concluded that no market disruption existed. She did suggest that if the president were to impose a remedy, it should be in the form of a tariff-rate quota for three years: no duty on the first 60 million pounds of honey and a 10 percent ad valorem tariff for imports exceeding 60 million pounds.

President Clinton rejected relief in this case. He offered three reasons. First, even if higher tariffs were imposed on Chinese honey, unaffected nations could increase their honey imports. Second, the total costs to consumers outweighed the benefit to domestic bee-keepers. Finally, the president felt that protectionist action would contravene his policy of free trade. Thus, Clinton found that the ITC's recommendations were not in the "national economic interest of the United States."[3]

Ammonium Paratungstate and Tungstic Acid from China

China received most-favored-nation status in 1980; Chinese imports became eligible for the preferred lower column 1 tariff rate as opposed to punitive tariff rates of Smoot-Hawley.[4] Soon China began trading tungsten at modest levels and, from 1980 to 1983, reached a 3 percent market share. By 1984, it began exporting tungsten more aggressively into the United States. By 1986, China's market share had rocketed to 17 percent while the domestic market declined. Offering lower prices than domestic producers, China's import success led to an ITC investigation that culminated in the initial use of section 406 quotas to curtail Communist imports.

The tungsten products under investigation, ammonium para-tungstate and tungstic acid, were intermediate ingredients in the manufacture of tungsten powders. Domestically, tungstic acid was not sold commercially. Virtually all the domestic product was consumed by the producer and used in the production of ammonium paratungstate.

During the early 1980s, the domestic tungsten industry was in a state of flux. World consumption of tungsten waned after the 1970s, as demand subsided for downstream products such as tool steels, armaments, and electrical products. Domestic consumption bottomed out between 12 million and 13 million pounds in 1982 and 1983. In 1984, consumption rose to 19.4 million pounds but subsided to 14.3 million pounds in 1986. Domestic capacity utilization for this period rose from about 46 percent in 1983 to a peak of 77 percent in 1986 and then dropped back to 46 percent. Despite the bell-shaped cycle of bust, boom, and bust, the industry as a whole suffered operating losses throughout the period, and industry employment dropped by 31 percent.

The ITC found that the decline of domestic tungsten demand contributed to the industry's material injury. The rapid increase of Chinese tungsten imports, however, was a significant cause of that injury. Specifically, the imported tungsten won market share despite declining consumption by undercutting prices. "The ratio of the cost of goods sold to net sales increased steadily after 1984 suggesting that prices were being depressed relative to costs, even while the raw material component of those costs was declining."[5] In this instance, prices for imported Chinese tungsten declined 71 percent more than prices for domestically produced tungsten. Imports increased in both market share and volume throughout the period.

The ITC concluded that the domestic industry was experiencing market disruption due to the Chinese imports. Accordingly, the commission recommended market share quotas restricting imports to 7.5 percent of domestic consumption for five years. The recommendation included a floor figure that allowed for annual imports based on the average of annual import amounts for 1982 to 1984. The commission rejected tariff relief because "we found it difficult to predict how much of a tariff increase the PRC is likely to absorb."[6] Two concurring commissioners proposed a more generous market share quota of 17.2 percent; another suggested that the quota be fixed at more stringent 1984 levels.

For the first and only time since section 406 came into existence, the president chose to grant relief to the domestic industry. While acknowledging China's status as a most-favored-nation trading partner, President Reagan nonetheless maintained that the "present agreement for orderly trade is within the parameters of the safeguard measures envisioned by the bilateral trade agreement."[7] Under threat of section 406 sanctions, China agreed to limit tungsten imports to 1982–1984 levels for five years in an orderly marketing agreement.[8]

Anhydrous Ammonia from the Soviet Union

In 1973, Occidental Petroleum Corporation and the Soviet Union signed a countertrade agreement to build ammonia plants with loans financed by the Export-Import Bank.[9] Occidental contributed technology to establish the facilities. In return, it received the exclusive right to purchase and market the Soviet ammonia for twenty years for use in domestic fertilizer. At its conception, the project received the blessing of the Nixon administration and was hailed as a breakthrough in U.S.-Soviet relations.[10]

In 1978, the Soviet plants began production and shipped 300,000 tons of ammonia into the United States. The next year, shipments increased to 1 million tons, with 2 million expected in 1981. This represented a domestic market share of 2 percent in 1978 and 6 percent in 1979; the figure was expected to rise to 12 percent in 1981. Alleging a market disruption, several domestic ammonia producers petitioned for import relief under section 406 in 1979.

In 1978, the ammonia industry was in a weakened state owing to fluctuating natural gas prices and underutilized capacity after significant capital expansion in the mid-1970s. Operating profit for domestic ammonia producers fell from $316 million in 1976 to $149 million in 1977 and $10 million in 1978. From mid-1978 to mid-1979, the industry incurred a $44 million loss.

A three-commissioner majority of the ITC found that the increase in imports created a threat to domestic producers that required protection from Soviet ammonia imports. In particular, the commissioners found that Occidental's forward-pricing contracts placed domestic producers at a disadvantage in the face of escalating costs for raw materials.

The commission also reasoned that "the tremendous growth in Soviet productive capacity over a short 5-year period does not appear to reflect either Soviet or world market needs." The ITC cited a CIA report warning that Soviet ammonia production would destabilize the world market in the 1980s. The commission invoked national security, stating that "the ability of the United States to maintain its highly efficient agricultural productive enterprise is vital to our economy and to our national welfare as well as the free world which is also the beneficiary of our agricultural efficiency."[11]

Commissioners Stern and Alberger dissented from the opinion of the majority. They observed that the industry was poised for a major recovery in 1979. Following an ammonia boom in the mid-1970s, many producers upgraded to larger plants with modern technology to increase their efficiency and competitiveness. This expanded the domestic capacity for ammonia production by 44 percent. The combination of large capital expenditures, dramatic increases in energy costs, and weakened demand led to a bust period from 1975 to 1978. The overwhelming majority of plants that closed during the bust, however, were of the older, outmoded variety. What was left, the commissioners asserted, was a lean and efficient industry.

Stern and Alberger found that while the industry experienced material injury, the injury had been present since 1975, well before the influx of Soviet imports. "After full consideration of all the available information in this case, we have not been able to find any credible shred of evidence that would link the Soviet imports to the material injury the domestic industry has experienced or may continue to experience."[12] They further opined that predictions of future prices, including predictions that Occidental's forward contracts would undercut domestic producers, were pointless and ill-founded in an industry experiencing large price fluctuations.

Additionally, if Congress included the "increasing imports" requirement to prevent Communist products from flooding the market, then Soviet ammonia imports did not qualify as increasing: "We cannot believe that the notion of flooding contemplates slowly-increasing market penetration over a long period of time."[13]

Finally, Stern and Alberger reasoned that Soviet imports would not significantly affect the domestic industry. Imports in general had grown every year except 1976; thus, eliminating ammonia imports from one nation would most likely result in an increase in imports from another country.

Presidential Action and the Second ITC Investigation

President Carter declined to act on the ITC findings, citing the national interest. He reversed a few months later, however, and imposed interim quotas after the Soviet invasion of Afghanistan "altered the international economic conditions." He then asked the ITC to institute another investigation.

This time, in a 3–2 determination, the ITC found no market disruption, stating that no new issues had been presented since the previous investigation. In fact, the recovery that Commissioners Stern and Alberger predicted appeared to exceed their expectations. Capacity utilization in the domestic industry had risen twelve percentage points since 1978, and the decline in profitability had reversed. With a finding of no market disruption, the quotas on Soviet ammonia imports ceased.[14]

Clothespins from China, Romania, and Poland

In 1978, the Clothespin and Veneer Products Association petitioned for relief under section 406 from wood spring clothespins imported from Poland, Romania, and China. Because an ITC investigation under section 406 can apply to only one Communist country at a time, three investigations were launched concurrently.

Between 1975 and 1977, clothespin imports flooded the domestic market. Capacity utilization of domestic producers fell by 17 percent from 1973 to 1978, and the industry profit margin dropped from 8.3 percent to 0.7 percent. The ITC quickly dismissed the cases involving Poland and Romania from consideration for section 406 relief because imports from those countries merely fluctuated or increased moderately.

The investigation against China, however, continued. The commission found several instances where Chinese imports displaced sales from domestic producers. Furthermore, China had built a 20 percent market share from scratch in four years and depressed domestic prices with its cheaper imports. Thus, Chinese clothespins caused a market disruption.

The ITC recommended that President Carter impose quotas. Carter declined, however, citing that Chinese imports accounted for only 27 percent of clothespin imports. If Chinese imports were curtailed, other nations would be likely to fill excess demand with imports of their own. Industry relief would thus be better suited to action under section 201.

In 1979, Carter imposed a tariff on clothespin imports under section 201. This tariff applied to all importers of clothespins, not just China. Taiwan, in particular, posed the greatest threat to the domestic industry; between 1976 and 1979, its share of imports jumped from 47 percent to 88 percent. The ITC determined that "we are convinced that the domestic clothespin industry could be viable, although we believe it is unlikely that its prices will match those of low-valued imports for the foreseeable future."[15]

Timetable for Section 406 Action

A petition for relief under section 406 may come from a domestic firm, trade association, union, or group of workers that is representative of the industry. It may also be filed on the request of the president or the U.S. trade representative or "upon resolution of either the Committee on Ways and Means of the House of Representatives or the Committee on Finance of the Senate." The ITC may also institute an investigation on its own. After receiving a petition for section 406 relief, the ITC must issue an initial preliminary determination within 45 days whether to pursue the investigation. The ITC then must issue a second preliminary determination within 115 days for most cases or 165 days for the complicated cases. This second determination must show either a positive or negative finding of market disruption. A third determination follows within 75 days or, if the commission chooses to extend the investigation, 135 days. At this point, a negative determination terminates the investigation. With a positive finding, however, the ITC must issue a final determination within 45 days in routine cases or 75 days in complicated cases.

Investigations Finding No Market Disruption

Fans from China. On May 22, 1992, Lasko Metal Products, Inc., petitioned the ITC to investigate Chinese imports of oscillating table, floor, and wall fans.[16] The commission scheduled public hearings and began preliminary proceedings. On June 30, however, Lasko withdrew its petition and asked the ITC to terminate the investigation. The company claimed that this move promoted its "interest in maintaining good relations with its customers" because they found "the time and effort needed to respond to the Commission's questionnaires burdensome."[17] The ITC granted the request on acquiescence of the only other domestic fan producer.

Ferrosilicon from the Soviet Union. Between 1982 and 1983, the domestic ferrosilicon industry's production and employment fell by about 40 percent. In the latter half of 1983, the Soviet Union began exporting ferrosilicon to the United States in quantities that represented 3.8 percent of domestic production. At the request of the U.S. trade representative, the ITC began an investigation. In this case, the commission found that Soviet imports were increasing rapidly and the industry was experiencing material injury. In a 4–1 ruling, however, the commission concluded that the Soviet imports were not the cause of injury. Rather, the industry's condition stemmed from other conditions in the market. The commission also found that the imports were not a significant cause of a threat of material injury. It explained that threat of injury exists only when "injury, although not yet existing, is clearly imminent if import trends continued unabated." According to the commission, the industry was poised for a recovery that would be largely unaffected by the modest amount of Soviet imports.

Chairman Eckes disagreed with the majority, calling Soviet ferrosilicon imports a "classic case of market disruption." He stated that ferrosilicon was not a nonessential agricultural product, but a raw material to vital industries with "far-reaching implications for national defense and this country's industrial base." Eckes further observed that Congress passed section 406 to prevent the United States from becoming dependent on Communist imports for vital materials. In light of rising Soviet market share, evidence of imports underselling the domestic industry, and testimony blaming lost sales on Soviet imports, Eckes found a market disruption.[18]

Canned Mushrooms from China. In this section 406 investigation,[19] the ITC split evenly in a 2–2 vote on whether a market disruption existed in the canned mushroom industry. At the time, the domestic industry was enjoying some measure of relief under section 201, and canned mushroom imports were declining. Nevertheless, Commissioners Frank and Haggart recommended tariffs on the Chinese canned mushrooms that replaced Korean and Taiwanese imports, thereby nullifying previously imposed escape-clause tariffs. They reasoned, "Had not Hong Kong, Macao, and China increased their lower-priced exports to the U.S. market, domestic producers might have been able to generate higher profits and sustain greater adjustment efforts."[20] The ITC determined that even though the mushrooms under investigation were grown in China, section 406 relief could apply only to a Communist country. Therefore, imports from Hong Kong and Macao could not be included in the section 406 investigation.

Commissioners Eckes and Stern argued that the industry experienced no material injury. They observed a tenuous relationship between the health of the domestic industry and Chinese imports. During the period in which Chinese imports increased the most, domestic producers enjoyed a rise in profits. Moreover, the fluctuating employment levels in the industry could be attributed to the shifting productivity of workers. Under section 406, a tie vote of the ITC results in a negative determination.

Critics of section 406 assert that the act is largely ineffective. This criticism is often based on the limited attempts of domestic producers to invoke the act, while nearly fifty cases have been instituted pursuant to section 201, ten times more than all section 406 cases. Another criticism is that the act is moribund because of the chief executive's reluctance to grant relief.

The flood of Communist imports predicted by the authors of the act has largely not occurred. Recent developments have curtailed the number of Communist countries that are subject to the act. Presently, section 406 may credibly be targeted only at China. As imports from China continue to grow, they have been met with antidumping actions, requiring no exercise of executive discretion or expenditures of political capital.

7

Imports and National Security

Section 232 of the Trade Expansion Act of 1962 permits the president to "to adjust the imports" of an article "so that such imports will not threaten to impair the national security."[1] The adjustment typically comes in the form of quotas or voluntary restraint agreements (VRAs). The petition of a domestic industry or the motion of the Department of Commerce or another agency may initiate an investigation under section 232. After determining the impact on national security of the imports under investigation, the secretary of commerce releases his recommendations to the president. Similarly to investigations under section 406, the president has the discretion to decide what actions, if any, will be taken to adjust the imports on national security grounds.

In investigating imports under section 232, the secretary of commerce considers (1) the quantity, quality, and availability of imports; (2) the requirements of the nation's defense and civilian sectors; (3) the maximum domestic mobilization capacity; (4) the impact of foreign competition on the economic welfare of an essential domestic industry; and (5) other factors relevant to the unique circumstances.

Case Studies

A typical section 232 investigation involved the imports of thermoplastic injection molding machines. The Domestic Injection Molding Machinery Trade Group of the Society of the Plastics Industry of Washington, D.C., petitioned the Department of Commerce on January 11, 1988, to investigate under section 232 to determine the effect of imports of thermoplastic injection molding machines on national security.

On February 29, the Department of Commerce accepted the trade group's application. The articles to be investigated were both horizontal and vertical plastic injection molding machines. These machines were used to manufacture a host of goods ranging in complexity from ballpoint pens to radar equipment parts. They were considered indispensable in the production of fighter aircraft and submarine parts. The U.S. industry dropped from seventeen manufacturers in 1978 to only seven in 1988.

In its petition, the trade group asserted that "import penetration has drastically endangered the health of the injection molding machinery industry . . . [and the] continued and uncontrolled importation [of injection molding machines] is a threat to the national security."[2]

On January 11, 1989, the Department of Commerce submitted its investigation report to the president. The investigation determined that, at the present time, supplies of plastic injection molding machines could meet anticipated requirements during a national security emergency. Robert Mosbacher, the secretary of commerce, concluded that the machines were not being imported into the United States in quantities or under circumstances that threatened national security. Accordingly, the secretary recommended that the president take no action to adjust imports. On February 17, 1989, President George Bush announced that he accepted the department's recommendation.

Although no action was taken under section 232, Secretary of Commerce Mosbacher, in a February 17, 1989, statement, recommended three steps to support the industry's ability to respond to current and future defense requirements. The department's National Institute of Standards and Technology was to work with the domestic manufacturers to develop sensors and to improve understanding of the molding process. This step was to help "evaluate and control the microstructure and production accuracies of injection molded parts while still in the mold, increasing the industry's productivity and reliability." Second, the secretary of commerce announced a joint program with the Department of Justice to identify opportunities for American industry, including the plastic injection molding industry, to strengthen its international competitiveness. Third, Mosbacher urged Defense Department officials to confer with the domestic manufacturers to explore revitalization efforts.[3]

Uranium

Another investigation under section 232 involved the uranium industry. On December 30, 1988, the secretary of energy, John Herrington, requested the secretary of commerce to conduct an investigation to determine the effects of uranium imports on national security. The articles subject to investigation included uranium ores and concentrates, metals, oxides, and hexafluorides.

This request was prompted by section 170(b) (42 U.S.C. 2210b) of the Atomic Energy Act of 1954. The secretary of energy must determine whether (1) contracts or options for foreign uranium account for more than 37.5 percent of domestic requirements for two consecutive years or (2) the level of contract or options for foreign uranium threaten national security. If an affirmative determination is reached on either point, section 170(b) requires the secretary of energy to request an investigation.

At the time of the investigation, U.S. utilities imported 43.8 percent of their uranium requirements in 1986 and 51.1 percent in 1987. Uranium is absolutely essential to the operation of the navy's nuclear-powered fleet. Enriched uranium is a key component of the nation's nuclear weapons arsenal. In the civilian sector, nuclear power plants supplied almost 20 percent of U.S. electricity requirements in 1988. In this respect, uranium plays a critical role in the energy independence and security of the United States.[4]

Investment as well as production of uranium experienced a severe decline in the late 1980s. Employment in the industry had also dropped. Domestic prices for uranium had fluctuated since 1964, and exports had declined because of lower-cost competition in the world market.[5] The domestic industry's competitiveness deteriorated in the late 1980s because of the easily accessible and richer deposits available elsewhere. Canadian deposits, for example, may contain up to 60 percent ore. U.S. mines may be considered commercially feasible with deposits of less than 1 percent content.

In addition, because nuclear power was not utilized to the extent predicted during the early stages of the industry, demand for uranium to generate electricity was lower than anticipated. Too large an inventory and market prices often lower than U.S. production costs also plagued the U.S. market.

The investigation revealed that, in a national security emergency, defense requirements could be met through stockpiles of finished material supplemented by natural uranium held at Department of Energy enrichment plants for defense needs. Nondefense needs could be filled with U.S. production and inventories, imports from allies such as Canada and Australia, and reprocessing of uranium ore.[6]

The secretary of commerce submitted his report to the president on September 26, 1989. The secretary had determined that available supplies of uranium could meet anticipated requirements during a national security emergency. Uranium was not being imported in such quantities or under such circumstances as to threaten national security. On October 16, 1989, the president accepted the recommendation.

Antifriction Bearings

The Anti-Friction Bearing Manufacturers Association sought relief under section 232. Antifriction bearings are considered essential in any metal product with moving parts and are therefore necessary for manufacturing defense products. Direct and indirect military consumption of bearings accounts for approximately one-fifth of U.S. consumption. Accordingly, the Department of Commerce considered a "viable domestic bearings industry as a key element of the defense manufacturing base."[7]

In its petition, the association asserted that "the domestic bearings industry is in a state of serious decline . . . [and unless action is taken] the domestic industry's ability to supply military and related commercial needs is seriously endangered."[8] The petitioner requested that quotas be established for 0–34 percent of the U.S. market for the various bearing product categories.

On July 28, 1987, the Department of Commerce accepted the application requesting an investigation. The articles investigated included all ball and roller bearings, bearing parts, and mounted bearings.

The Commerce investigation found that projected supply could meet national security requirements in eight categories. Thus, imports did not threaten national security in those categories of bearings. Supply shortfalls, however, were found in seven other categories of bearings. Therefore, an additional investigation of supply availability and market trends was conducted for these seven categories. In five of them, imports did not pose a threat. The Department of Commerce determined that shortfalls possibly attributable to high levels of import penetration existed in two of the fifteen bearing categories under review: regular precision ball bearings under 30 millimeters and regular precision bearings 30–100 millimeters.

Before issuing any recommendation to the president, the department considered what steps the government was already taking to address the industry's problems. The Department of Defense had adopted a federal acquisition regulation requiring domestic procurement of ball bearings under 30 millimeters used in military products. Defense published draft regulations to expand the existing federal acquisition regulation to cover all bearings used in military products. In addition, the Defense Department was undertaking other initiatives to improve the industry's production base and ability to meet national security requirements.

The investigation by the Department of Commerce found that the domestic bearings industry could meet most but not all national security requirements in the event of a major conventional war. Furthermore, because imports continued to pose significant challenges to domestic manufacturers in several product lines, domestic production capabilities could further erode.

The secretary of commerce therefore recommended that the president defer making a finding in this investigation or taking any action until the effect of the aforementioned initiatives on the bearing industry's ability to meet national security requirements had been evaluated by the Departments of Commerce and Defense. The president announced the assessments of the departments on November 28, 1988:

1. Current U.S. demand for bearings was at its highest point in many years.

2. The U.S. industry had benefited from the increase in domestic demand and had been operating at close to 100 percent of capacity for the past six months in most bearing categories.

3. The U.S. industry had recently attracted significant investment from domestic and foreign producers, partly because production costs in this country dropped below those of European and Japanese competitors.[9]

The investigation determined that the restriction of Defense purchases to domestic producers could mean $40–50 million to those suppliers, as well as a reversal of any increase in defense-related bearings imports. The president accepted the recommendation that no action was necessary.[10]

Integrated Circuit Ceramic Packages

On November 10, 1992, Coors Electronic Package Company and Ceramic Process Systems Corporation jointly requested the Department of Commerce to initiate a section 232 investigation to determine the effects on national security of imports of integrated-circuit ceramic packages. Ceramic semiconductor packages are a key component of the microelectronic element of virtually every military system. One survey identified 113 distinct defense systems that require these packages, including the Patriot, Tomahawk, and Trident missiles; the Comanche helicopter; and the F-14 and F-18 aircraft. Industry experts estimate that direct and indirect military consumption accounts for approximately 20 percent of total U.S. consumption of ceramic packages.[11]

U.S. production of ceramic packages declined an estimated 60 percent on a unit basis and 24 percent on a value basis between 1990 and 1992. Two-thirds of the products in the domestic market was controlled by one foreign company. Such a serious dependency on a foreign supplier raised national security implications.

As part of their petition, Coors and Ceramic Process requested "(1) Government support for additional research and development leading to commercialization of advanced materials; (2) qualification assistance to enable domestic suppliers to participate in existing military programs being supplied with ceramic packages from Japan; and (3) any (additional) relief the President deems appropriate to stop the further deterioration of the U.S. ceramic package industry."[12]

On November 18, 1992, the Department of Commerce formally accepted the application and initiated an investigation. The department was assisted by the interagency community, "including the Departments of Defense, Energy, Justice, Labor, State and the Treasury; the Central Intelligence Agency; the Council of Economic Advisers; the National Aeronautics and Space Administration; the Office of Management and Budget; and the Office of the U.S. Trade Representative."[13]

On August 16, 1993, Commerce submitted its investigation report to the president. The secretary concluded that imports were not impairing national security. The secretary would review the financial and production status of the domestic industry in one year, and if the situation warranted, another national security investigation would be initiated. Despite the negative finding, Secretary Ron Brown proposed that President Clinton adopt several programs to enhance the competitiveness of the domestic industry:

1. Establish a Manufacturing Center of Excellence headed by the Navy Department to address the production deficiencies of U.S. producers

2. Create a Materials Research and Development Program to be led by Commerce's National Institute of Standards and Tech-

nology (NIST) and the Energy Department's Oak Ridge National Laboratory

3. Establish a Product and Process Qualification Program directed by NIST and the Energy Department's Sandia National Laboratory

4. Create a Government-Industry Ceramic Packaging Working Group to coordinate the first three activities and ensure the continued commitment of all parties.[14]

This four-part plan was an attempt to revitalize the domestic industry, which declined in profitability, capacity, and investment between 1990 and 1992.

Crude Oil and Petroleum Products

On January 24, 1994, the Department of Commerce denied a section 232 petition by the Independent Petroleum Association of America to reduce oil imports. The association had asked President Clinton to take action under Section 232 and a January 3, 1989, finding by former president Reagan that oil imports were a threat to national security.

The 1989 Investigation. The Department of Commerce initiated an investigation in December 1987 in response to a petition filed by the National Energy Security Committee. On completion of the investigation, the secretary of commerce concluded that U.S. energy security had substantially improved since the last section 232 petroleum investigation in 1979. Rising oil imports, declining domestic oil production, and growing global dependence on potentially insecure sources of supply, however, raised a number of concerns, including, for example, vulnerability to a major supply disruption. The Department of Commerce determined that the maintenance of U.S. access to adequate supplies of petroleum was essential to our nation's "economic security, foreign policy flexibility, and defense preparedness."[15] Accordingly, the secretary of commerce found that petroleum imports threatened national security.

Despite this threat, the secretary recommended that no action to adjust imports under section 232 (such as an oil import fee) be taken because "such action would not be cost effective and, in the long run, would impair rather than enhance national security." This decision was also based, in large part, on the Reagan administration's

detailed program to improve energy security, which was transmitted to Congress in May 1987 (only portions of which were acted on
by Congress), and the drastic increase in the strategic petroleum
reserve from 108 million barrels in 1981 to over 555 million barrels
in 1989.[16]

Barry Carter, Commerce acting under secretary, explained the
denial: the statute required that a remedy be imposed no later than
fifteen days after a presidential finding. Carter explained that the
act did not "permit action to be initiated five years after such a determination, as IPAA seeks. If it did, the 15 day limitation would be
meaningless."[17]

Petition Seeking New Investigation. Disappointed with the
department's interpretation of the act, the Independent Petroleum
Association of America subsequently submitted a petition to Commerce on March 11, 1994, once again requesting an investigation to
determine the effects on national security of imports of crude oil
and petroleum products. On April 5, 1994, the department formally
accepted the application and initiated a new investigation.

Commerce considered several measures, including a series of
tax increases on petroleum product imports reaching twelve cents
per gallon by the year 2000, to help counterbalance the advantages
of foreign refiners from operating under less restrictive environmental, health, and safety regulations. The domestic industry recommended that a seven-cent-per-gallon import fee on refined products
start in 1995 and rise one cent per gallon annually through the year
2000. Charles Dunlap, president and CEO of Crown Central Petroleum Corporation, stated that "due to the high cost of environmental compliance, the U.S. refining industry is expected to lose another
10% of its capacity resulting from refinery shutdowns in the next
three to five years."[18] He added that, in the 1980s, the number of
domestic refineries dropped from a high of 315 to only 184. In 1994,
the U.S. imported approximately 50 percent of its oil. Dunlap predicted a 10 percent rise in U.S. dependence on oil imports by the end
of the century.

An analysis by the Petroleum Industry Research Foundation
Inc. (Pirinc) found that "any measure imposed to achieve a significant reduction in oil imports from their current or projected level
under existing market conditions would raise the price of oil to the
point where it would cause measurable damage to the U.S. economy."[19]
Alternatively, Pirinc Chairman John Lichtblau suggested that

a proactive policy to stimulate additional oil and gas drilling through tax incentives and royalty waivers for specifically defined new wells, as well as removal of existing federal and state off-shore acreage restrictions, could be viewed as being in the national interest—not because of its potential impact on oil imports but because of its significant real economic impact on a core regional industry.[20]

The logic behind this proposal was that, if properly designed, these actions would not represent a cost to the U.S. taxpayer over time since the "additional production would generate additional taxable revenues" and thus the policy would reward only actual drilling. Conversely, in the case of a price increase through import restrictions, the "amounts allocated for drilling remain at the discretion of the producer. The only certain thing would be that prices for all consumers would rise."[21]

In a December 29, 1995, report, Commerce Secretary Ron Brown advised President Clinton that, while reliance on imported oil did threaten national security, the economic costs of imposing a tariff were too severe. Agreeing with the Department of Commerce recommendation, on February 16, 1995, President Clinton declined to invoke section 232 to impose a tariff on oil imports. The president asserted that any potential harm caused by U.S. dependence on imported oil would be dealt with better by increasing domestic production and decreasing consumption. Clinton noted that "while reliance on imports of crude oil and refined petroleum products threatens the nation's security . . . [the administration will] . . . continue its present efforts to improve U.S. energy security, rather than adopt a specific import mechanism."[22]

Machine Tools

On March 10, 1983, the National Machine Tool Builders' Association petitioned the Department of Commerce to determine the effect of imports of machine tools on national security. Machine tools are used to produce ships, planes, tanks, missiles, transport vehicles, and other armament used by the armed forces.

In its petition, the domestic industry requested that Commerce "limit imports of both metal-cutting and metal-forming tools to 17.5 percent of domestic consumption, measured by value" for five years. The industry asserted that the Japanese government "created a cartel to manufacture and export machine tools, and that the Japanese government massively subsidizes its machine tool industry, enabling it to penetrate the U.S. market significantly."[23]

In February 1984, Secretary of Commerce Malcolm Baldrige reported to the president that imports posed a national security threat in several product lines. President Reagan requested Baldrige to review his findings in light of new planning guidelines being developed by the National Security Council.

In March 1985, Secretary Baldrige submitted a report incorporating the new planning guidance. Despite this report's conclusion that imports in seven of eighteen types did threaten security, several White House staff reportedly opposed such a ruling as setting a bad precedent.[24] Additionally, opponents of relief asserted that it would further strain U.S.- Japan relations and would make the administration look decidedly protectionist and that machine tool orders, in any event, were increasing.[25]

President Reagan chose not to grant relief under section 232. But he did announce an intention to negotiate VRAs with major exporters of machine tools and to revitalize the domestic industry. The president entered into voluntary restraint agreements on machine tool imports with Taiwan, Japan, West Germany, and Switzerland.[26] These VRAs were later renewed in 1992 by President Bush.

In addition to seeking import curbs, the president created a domestic action plan to help the industry by ordering the following steps:

1. The industry will be integrated "more fully" into the military procurement process. Companies will receive "more timely" information on military programs and Pentagon manufacturing requirements so that they can participate at an earlier stage in the procurement process.

2. Capabilities that support national defense will be modernized by Pentagon programs to improve productivity and advance technology.

3. The industry will receive up to $5 million a year over the next three years in federal matching funds to support a private-sector technology center for advances in manufacturing and design.

4. The attorney general and other agencies will investigate the potential for cooperative research and development in industry.

5. The secretary of commerce will monitor industry's performance on an annual basis, particularly steps to improve production capabilities and competitive position.[27]

Unlike the situation with other trade investigations such as antidumping or escape clause cases, section 232 investigations offer little room for economic analysis. The determination focuses on the national security implications of the product in question. No question is asked concerning the trade practices of the exporters. Additionally, the economic conditions of a particular domestic industry are irrelevant unless that industry can be linked to national security.

As demonstrated in the cases discussed above, a petitioner's chances for relief under section 232 are slim. As the case studies indicate, however, a petitioner may successfully use section 232 to draw attention to the condition of the domestic industry. Whether the product is machine tools or plastic molding or ceramic chips, an unsuccessful petitioner will not necessarily go home empty-handed. Rather, the type of assistance sought may come outside the rubric of section 232. Government grants for additional research and development and increased government procurement are more easily obtained by a domestic industry than quotas. These consolation prizes may outweigh the relief originally sought under section 232.

8
Protection of Intellectual Property

In terms of statutory language, section 337 of the Tariff Act of 1930 is the most sweeping trade measure in the American arsenal. In day-to-day practice, it has proved one of the most narrowly focused. The narrow applications, however, should not reflect on the statute's importance. This section's focus on new technologies and other forms of intellectual property, combined with the uncompromising nature of the remedy, has made it one of the most important and effective trade measures available to a domestic industry.

Scope of the Statute

The International Trade Commission administers section 337. On the filing of a complaint, the ITC investigates alleged "unfair methods of competition and unfair acts in the importation of articles . . . the threat or effect of which is to destroy or substantially injure a domestic industry in the United States."[1]

Over the years, over 90 percent of the section 337 cases brought to the ITC have involved an alleged violation of a U.S. intellectual property right: a patent, copyright, or registered trademark. In most section 337 cases, the allegations have been of a closely related sort, such as false designation of origin, palming off a product as that of another manufacturer, infringement of trade dress, and so forth.

In light of this history, Congress amended the statute in 1988 to make the infringement remedy explicit and to eliminate the injury requirement in infringement cases. Congress essentially presumed that the owner of intellectual property is injured by its infringement. Moreover, in contrast to infringement of a patent, copyright, or registered trademark, many other claims brought under section 337 involve injury as an element. A claim of palming off, for example, requires showing that consumers are likely to confuse the palmed off imports with the domestic product—a form of injury. From this perspective, therefore, all claims under section

94

337 are treated on an equal footing even though the statutory requirements differ.

Several cases over the years have demonstrated section 337's broad scope and ITC willingness to deploy the statute in creative ways. In 1934, the ITC (then the Tariff Commission) held that section 337 barred the importation of a good that, though not covered by a patent, was produced according to a process patented in the United States. The case was overturned on appeal, but Congress reinstated the commission's view by an amendment to section 337 a few years later. Congress did not pass an analogous amendment to the patent laws until 1988. Thus, importation of products manufactured by a patented process was a violation of the trade laws but not of the patent laws.

Also under the rubric of section 337, the commission has considered claims alleging antitrust violations, misappropriation of trade secrets, product disparagement, and false advertising—all involving imports into the United States. In 1984, the ITC found a violation based on the gray-market importation of batteries, that is, batteries produced abroad pursuant to a valid trademark license and then imported into the United States in violation of that license. Ultimately, the president rejected the ITC's decision in light of pending initiatives in the area of gray-market goods. An appeal from the ITC's decision, dismissed as moot, left open the question of section 337 scope in that area.

In 1990, the ITC rejected a section 337 case involving the importation of recombinant erythropoietin, a drug that is used for certain types of blood disorders and is produced by genetically altered organisms. The ITC held that the statute does not cover the imports, because neither the product nor the process of making it was covered by a U.S. patent, although the cells of the organisms were alleged to be covered by a valid U.S. patent. Whether this decision reflects a growing rigidity on the part of the ITC is not clear. The ITC focused on the aspect of patent infringement, and clearly neither the imports nor the manufacturing process was patented. The commission did not appear to rely on the broader language barring unfair acts or methods of competition. Conversely, the commission would not likely ever give section 337 the full scope that its language regarding unfair acts would seem to allow.

In section 337 cases not involving intellectual property, the complainant must establish injury to a domestic industry. Injury may be shown through the volume of offending imports, loss of market share, underpricing, lost sales, price suppression, and declining sales, profits, and employment. Rising inventory levels and an inability to raise prices to meet production costs are other factors the ITC considers in evaluating injury.

Whether the complainant must show injury or not, in every section 337 case the complainant must show that a domestic industry exists; that is, that the section 337 remedy would protect U.S. economic activity. A domestic industry qualified to bring an intellectual property claim under section 337 must have "significant investment in plant or equipment; significant employment of labor or capital; or substantial investment in its exploitation, including engineering, research and development and licensing." Disney, for example, may license the production of Mickey Mouse toys to a Canadian firm. The Canadian firm produces the Mickey Mouse toys in Singapore. If the licensed Disney toys are forced to compete with infringing toys imported from Pakistan, Disney could bring a section 337 case. Disney's licensing operations would constitute a domestic industry under section 337. Thus, the existence of significant economic activity in the United States—but not necessarily manufacturing facilities—is the dispositive factor in establishing a domestic industry. This flexibility recognizes the importance of licensing and research-related activities to the domestic economy.

Still, in almost any section 337 cases, and particularly in patent cases, the domestic industry requirement means that the complainant or its licensee must make or use in the United States the intellectual property allegedly infringed. This inquiry is specific. If a patent owner makes a product covered by some, but not all, the claims covered by a patent, for example, the owner may not bring a section 337 action with respect to imports covered by the unused claims. The patent owner may file a patent infringement lawsuit in federal court, however.

The domestic industry does not have to be U.S.- owned. Makita, a Japanese power tool manufacturer, for example, brought an action at the ITC asserting trademark infringement against U.S. importers and Taiwanese manufacturers. Makita was permitted to do so because it had engaged in "significant investment in plant and equipment and significant employment of labor and capital" in the United States for the product at issue; that is, it had established a domestic industry for that good. Several other foreign-owned companies have also used the ITC as a forum to combat patent infringement.

Conversely, in some investigations, the complainant and all respondents are domestic firms. Texas Instruments is believed to be the first U.S. company to use the statute solely against other American firms. Texas Instruments, the Dallas-based semiconductor and electronics company, charged five American manufacturers with violating section 337 by importing computer chips that violated the firm's patents. The ITC ultimately determined that the U.S. firms were infringing valid Texas Instruments patents.

The ITC oversaw twenty-seven section 337 investigations in 1993 (although not all of these were initiated or terminated in that year). Of these investigations, six were resolved by settlement agreements entered into by the parties or consent orders entered by the commission before the hearing. Four investigations were disposed of by settlement or consent orders after a hearing. In three instances, the investigations were terminated when the complainant withdrew the case. In two cases, the ITC reached final determinations that section 337 had been violated.

Remedies

Under section 337, the ITC may issue one or more of a number of remedies. The most potent is the general exclusion order. Pursuant to a general exclusion order, the U.S. Customs Service is directed by the ITC to bar the items described in the order from entry into the United States. This broad-based order bars not only items being imported by the respondents in the section 337 investigation; rather, any and all goods found to be in violation of the order are excluded, whatever their source. The general exclusion order thus bars the infringing import or other imports found to be in violation regardless of the identity, nationality, or location of the manufacturer or importer. In some cases, the ITC may limit its exclusion order to goods manufactured or imported by a particular entity. A limited exclusion order would not apply to imports from unnamed sources.

In deciding which type of exclusion order to issue, the ITC considers whether there is (1) a widespread pattern of unauthorized use infringing complainants' rights and (2) business conditions that indicate that foreign manufacturers other than respondents (that could be identified in a limited exclusion order) are likely to enter the U.S. market with infringing articles. In sum, the ITC is more likely to issue a general exclusion order in a case involving numerous respondents, a number of unidentified manufacturers, and easy entry into the production of infringing goods.

Another form of relief under section 337 is a cease-and-desist order. This order, unlike the exclusion order, is issued against individuals or firms in the United States. Cease-and-desist orders bar domestic entities from selling infringing imports held in inventory. The ITC has no authority, however, to bar the sale of infringing products manufactured in the United States.

Although intellectual property cases constitute the bulk of section 337 investigations, they are by no means the only cases investigated under the statute. In 1988, Aunyx, an American manufacturer of photocopier toner, charged Japan-based Canon with unfair trade practices. The U.S. firm alleged that Canon was disparaging its products in an attempt to monopolize the toner industry. An administrative law judge at the ITC ruled that Canon had violated section 337 by engaging in unfair acts and competition in the importation and sale of toner. According to the judge, these acts intended to restrain or monopolize trade and commerce in the United States. Although the ITC later reversed this decision, the application of the section to an antitrust case illustrates the statute's broad reach.

The ITC investigation of plastic food storage containers provides an interesting example of the application of section 337 to false advertising and passing off charges. The imported goods were described in their packaging as "interchangeable with Tupperware." Product testing demonstrated this to be false advertising; the imported goods were determined to be inferior to Tupperware. The determination that the infringing goods were "passing" as Tupperware was based on the appearance of the goods, the similarity in packaging of the imported goods to Tupperware packaging, and the use of the name Tupperware in advertising. Retailers selling the items asserted that they were selling Tupperware, and the advertising in question posed the question, "Why go to a Tupperware party?" The ITC issued a cease-and-desist order to prohibit future false advertising and "passing off." The ITC also issued an exclusion order prohibiting importation of the goods in the complained-of packaging.

Despite the numerous advantages of section 337, the act is not without its drawbacks. The ITC, for example, cannot award monetary damages. If a party seeking monetary damages meets the jurisdictional requirements, it may pursue an action in federal court simultaneously with its section 337 case.

OUII and the Public Interest

As discussed above, the typical complaint in a section 337 investigation asserts that the complainant owns a U.S. patent or other intellectual property right and that products infringing the intellectual property right are being imported into the United States. Complaints have involved products ranging from such cutting-edge products as computer chips or synthetic drugs to in-line roller skates or electric ride-on toys.

One unique aspect of section 337 proceedings is the commission's role. In most respects, once a case is initiated, the ITC is relatively passive. An ITC staff office, the Office of Unfair Import Investigations (OUII), represents the public interest in each investigation. This representation is particularly important in section 337 cases for two reasons. First, in section 337, more than in any other trade remedy, the investigation is most like a private litigation; that is, it is arranged primarily by the parties themselves (subject to the oversight of an ITC administrative law judge). Second, the determination of a remedy in a section 337 case is discretionary; the commission may choose between several alternatives, or the ITC may decline to take action against infringing goods or unfair business practices if such action would be contrary to the public interest (considering the impact of a remedy on consumers, competitive conditions in the United States economy, and the effect of production of like products in the United States). A principal function of the OUII staff, therefore, is to ensure that the case is put in a posture for the commission to make these determinations.

Relief is rarely denied because of public interest considerations, and then only in extreme cases. In *Certain Automatic Crankspin Grinders*,[2] for example, relief was denied in light of concern that the domestic industry would be unable to meet demand for critically needed engine parts. Similarly, in *Certain Inclined-Field Acceleration Tubes*,[3] relief was denied because the ITC determined that the patent rights at issue were outweighed by a public interest in the research that used the product. Each of these cases had unusually compelling facts.

Section 337 Procedures

The section 337 process begins with the filing of a complaint with the ITC (although, as in most trade matters, the party initiating the case consults with the ITC staff before a case is filed). The commissioners review the complaint for compliance with statutory and regulatory requirements. Within thirty days of filing, the ITC votes on whether to institute an investigation. Unless the complaint is defective on its face, the commission institutes an inquiry—rejections of complaints are exceedingly rare. Under section 337 (and standard patent practice), for example, only a patent owner or an exclusive licensee has standing to bring an action; a nonexclusive licensee does not. Thus, the commission would not institute a complaint brought by a nonexclusive licensee.

While section 337 cases resemble federal court litigation in many respects, the unique nature of the proceeding requires that the complaint be more detailed than the bare bones notice pleading permitted by the federal rules of civil procedure. A complainant must state a claim in detail, for example, and must provide information regarding the nature of its business activities. Perhaps most important, the complainant must identify all proposed respondents (foreign manufacturers and U.S. importers) believed to be in violation of the statute. This last requirement is needed because section 337 is a trade remedy; unlike in a federal court action, in which defendants must have some connection with the forum in which the court sits, a respondent in a section 337 case may be a foreign entity with no connection with the United States whatsoever. The ITC can name that entity as a respondent and provide that entity with notice of the case and an opportunity to appear and defend itself only if the complainant reveals all relevant information in its possession at the outset of the case.

If the ITC institutes a section 337 investigation, a notice is published in the *Federal Register,* and the matter is assigned to an administrative law judge (ALJ) for oversight of all prehearing and trial activity. The respondents named in the complaint are served with the complaint and a formal notice of initiation of the investigation. Notice is also sent to the respondents' embassies in Washington.

The respondent must answer the complaint within twenty days. The ALJ then holds a preliminary conference with the parties within forty-five days of institution. At this conference, the parties discuss a discovery schedule, including document production and the deposition of witnesses in the United States and abroad. OUII attorneys, of course, participate in this three-handed litigation and may take their own discovery.

Section 337 litigation is governed by the Administrative Procedures Act and ITC rules that track closely the federal rules of civil procedure. ALJs are not bound by the federal rules of evidence but tend to follow them, more or less. During the prehearing and discovery phase of the litigation, the ALJ rules on all procedural motions and issues any legal rulings required for the expeditious resolution of the case. These decisions may be appealed to the commission, but such appeals (not to mention successful appeals) are rare.

In a typical case, an ALJ holds an evidentiary hearing during the ninth month after institution of the investigation. After the hearing, the ALJ issues an extensive initial determination. This initial determination includes all findings of fact and conclusions of law on the issues raised in the case. The initial determination provides a road map for the ITC commissioners for their final determination.

Either of the parties may petition the ITC to review the initial determination within ten days of issuance. Alternatively, the ITC may review the initial determination on its own motion. Typically, the ITC defers to the ALJ's expertise in intellectual property matters, and on these issues the initial determination often becomes the ITC's final determination. The ITC commissioners usually take a closer look at policy issues raised in the investigations, such as the circumstances in which different remedies should be issued, the scope of the remedy, and the proper standard for sanctioning parties. If the ITC modifies or reverses the initial determination on these (or any other) issues, the commission issues its final determination reflecting those modifications.

If the ITC finds that there has been a violation of section 337, it considers whether to issue relief and, if so, in what form. Usually, the commission issues some form of relief, even if it is relatively mild in effect. If the ITC decides to grant relief, however, its decision is not immediately final. In those cases, its determination is sent to the president (acting through the Office of the U.S. Trade Representative) for review. The president may, within sixty days, veto or modify the remedy. If the president vetoes or modifies an ITC remedy, that decision is not subject to judicial review. If the ITC finds no violation of the statute or if the president allows a remedy to stand in whole or in part, then the ITC finding of a violation of a statute is subject to judicial review.

Presidential vetoes of ITC investigations regarding section 337 are extremely rare. Normally, the president vetoes an ITC decision only if the subject of the decision touches on an area of particular political sensitivity—which may be why the complainant brought the case in the first place. In most cases, however, the threat of a presidential veto is not a significant factor in a case.

Until Congress amended section 337 in 1994, the ITC was required to render a final determination within twelve months of the institution of an investigation (or eighteen months in a more complicated case). The statute became the subject of a complaint in the GATT on the ground that section 337 discriminated against imports; that is, domestic cases involving claims of infringement or other unfair trade practices identical to those brought under section 337 were not subject to such a stringent and onerous timetable. In response to the challenge, Congress deleted the statutory deadline but encouraged the commission to conduct section 337 investigations as expeditiously as possible. The ITC has adopted new procedures that, like the amended statute, do not impose a set deadline for completion of a case but thus far have resulted in final determinations issued within the time frame permitted under the earlier statute.

In some instances, complainants may seek temporary relief during the investigation, either out of necessity (for example, the life cycle of their product is relatively short) or for strategic reasons (such as to pressure the respondents into agreeing to an early trial date or to a quick settlement). Temporary relief is similar to a preliminary injunction in federal courts, and the standard for granting relief is similar to the federal court standard; that is, the complainant must show a likelihood of success on the merits and a balance of equities favors granting the relief. If the ITC grants temporary relief, it issues a remedy that terminates on the date a final determination is issued.

The ITC may also conduct enforcement proceedings in connection with outstanding section 337 remedies. In these proceedings, the ITC investigates whether the importation of a particular product circumvents or violates an existing exclusion order. If, for example, a section 337 investigation resulted in a final determination that certain imports infringe a valid U.S. patent, the ITC might issue a limited exclusion order barring importation of the infringing product of certain respondents. If the U.S. patent owner uncovered information suggesting that respondents had initiated production of infringing goods under another name or had made insubstantial changes to the goods to avoid enforcement of the ITC's remedy, the complainant could initiate an enforcement proceeding to expand the scope of the order to include the "new" products.

The ITC may also issue advisory opinions on whether activities do or would violate an outstanding commission order. In the first instance, the ITC staff often renders informal advice regarding the scope or meaning of an outstanding section 337 order. A party—usually a respondent—may request a formal advisory opinion regarding the scope of an order, which the commission issues following an administrative proceeding before an ALJ.

A final section 337 determination (except for an advisory opinion) may be appealed to the U.S. Court of Appeals for the Federal Circuit in Washington, D.C. In one instance, a section 337 decision reached the Supreme Court. If history is a guide, that will be the last Supreme Court involvement in section 337 matters for several generations.

Parties found to be in violation of ITC section 337 orders face civil penalties of up to $100,000 a day or twice the value of the imported articles.

Many of the unfair business practices complained of under section 337 could also be the subject of a lawsuit in a federal district court (or, in some cases, a state court). Actions are often filed simultaneously at the ITC and in federal court. Until the most recent statutory amendments, ITC and district court cases proceeded in tandem—although district judges often held their cases in abeyance pending the outcome of the ITC action. The recent amendments require district courts to hold their cases in abeyance and to accept the ITC's record after the section 337 case is concluded.

In most cases, one would expect the cases to yield similar results. Both substantive and procedural differences, however, can come into play. The outcome of a section 337 case, for example, might turn on the existence of a domestic industry, which would be irrelevant in an underlying infringement claim in federal court. Also, a section 337 case and a patent infringement action in a federal court would both be appealed to the federal circuit; in other circumstances, the district court and ITC decisions would be appealed to separate courts, which might not agree. Finally, the statute does not specify simultaneous ITC and state court proceedings. In many cases, however, parties find that section 337 provides superior relief.

One major advantage that section 337 cases have over federal or state court lawsuits is that the actions are similar to in rem actions. In rem actions are suits against particular goods, as distinguished from in personam actions, which are brought against a particular party.[4] The advantage of an in rem–like proceeding is that the complainant need not demonstrate a connection between the respondent and the federal or state forum in which the case is filed. In some cases, therefore, a party may be subject to ITC jurisdiction in a section 337 case, even if it has had no notice of the underlying section 337 investigation (although, as discussed above, efforts are made to ensure that this does not occur). This feature of section 337 is particularly important when the foreign respondents are numerous, unidentified, and have no connections to the United States—all of which would make a suit in federal court impossible. Moreover, if circumstances are such that the ITC issues a general exclusion order, the nature of a section 337 proceeding ensures that unnamed parties will not be able to circumvent the order by changing the identity or location of their operations.

Another advantage to section 337 investigations is speed. In most cases, a firm filing an ITC complaint is virtually assured of a quicker result than with a similar claim in a federal court. Furthermore, a successful complainant at the ITC gains the benefit of a government-enforced exclusion order. Successful litigants in private court actions must seek to have their orders enforced individually against infringers on a case-by-case basis. The aspect of government enforcement of section 337 removes this burden from the complainant.

9
Section 301 and Trade Retaliation

One of the most often mentioned of all U.S. trade laws is section 301 of the 1974 Trade Act.[1] This section provides for retaliatory actions against foreign states that unjustifiably burden or restrict U.S. commerce or deny U.S. rights under international trade agreements.[2] Under section 301, the U.S. trade representative can suspend or withdraw previously granted trade agreement concessions, impose retaliatory tariffs, or set quotas on imports from the offending state.[3] The USTR may also "enter into binding agreements" with foreign countries to eliminate a questionable practice, policy, burden, or restriction.[4] These agreements may provide the United States with compensatory trade benefits that need not necessarily benefit the aggrieved industry. If the "provision of such trade benefits is not feasible" for the aggrieved industry, a different industry may receive the benefits.[5]

Under section 301, actions by foreign states not violative of international legal rights of the United States may nonetheless be characterized as unreasonable. An act is unreasonable if it is "unfair and inequitable."[6] A consideration in this determination is whether the United States offers foreign nationals reciprocal opportunities.[7]

Section 301 is also designed to deter and punish unjustifiable practices that burden or restrict U.S. commerce.[8] An unjustifiable practice is one that violates or is inconsistent with the international legal rights of the United States.[9] Policies that deny U.S. firms national treatment in trade, service, or investment or fail to protect U.S. intellectual property are by statute unjustifiable.[10]

The most typical complaints under section 301 involve practices that deny U.S. firms access to foreign markets, restrict opportunities for direct investment, or do not adequately protect intellectual property. Section 301 sanctions, however, may also be imposed on states that violate workers' rights or engage in export targeting.[11]

The U.S. trade representative annually compiles a national trade estimate on foreign trade barriers.[12] This report is submitted to the president, the Senate Finance Committee, and committees of the House of Representatives. The targets of section 301 investigations come from this directory of foreign trade barriers; the number of pages devoted to a country indicates the likelihood that the state will be named as a section 301 target.[13]

Given the power and political pressure surrounding the section 301 process, the need for accurate information is obvious. The information-gathering process for the national trade estimate reports, however, is at best an inexact pursuit. In compiling the report, the USTR solicits information from U.S. embassies abroad and from the Departments of Commerce, Agriculture, Treasury, State, Labor, and Justice, as well as the National Security Council, the Council of Economic Advisers, and the Office of Management and Budget.[14] Private sector advisory committees also contribute information for the report.[15] Thus, in determining the existence and impact of foreign trade barriers, the USTR relies on corporations and individuals who stand to benefit directly from the finding or the exaggeration of such barriers.

A fundamental issue in the report is the determination of what exactly constitutes a trade barrier. According to the report, foreign trade barriers fall into eight distinct categories.[16] Included in this litany are "government-imposed measures and policies that restrict, prevent, or impede the international exchange of goods and services."[17]

The lists of practices that have been defined as barriers in the national trade estimate reports are too numerous to mention here. The report and threats of section 301 trade sanctions are often used as a bludgeon by U.S. manufacturers to gain access to markets that are closed as a matter of national policy.

The USTR, for example, has listed India's practice of not opening its lucrative insurance markets to foreign insurers.[18] All insurance in the $3 billion Indian market is issued by two state-operated firms: General Insurance Co. of India and Life Insurance Co. of India.[19] No one else may sell insurance in this market, not even Indian nationals.[20] It is difficult to discern the discrimination or unfair trade practice in such a market.

The USTR also assailed India's restrictive practices of foreign direct investment. Foreign investment in India may only control 40 percent of the equity in an Indian venture unless the firm is engaged in technology transfer or produces solely for export.[21] After an investigation, USTR Carla Hills determined on June 14, 1990, that India's regulation of the insurance market was an "unreasonable burden restricting U.S. commerce."[22] India refused to negotiate under the threat of U.S. retaliatory trade sanctions. Indeed, Indian Commerce Minister Arun Nehru commented: "Threats of retaliation are things of the medieval past. We don't negotiate under threat."[23] New Delhi lawmakers united in their refusal to bow to "U.S. blackmail" and stood fast to protect Indian sovereignty from U.S. pressures.

Presidential Involvement

Although investigation under section 301 has become commonplace, actual retaliation is seldom imposed. Typically, the negotiations between the USTR and the foreign state reach a breakthrough just short of the actual imposition of sanctions. The president, however, has retaliated under section 301 against several trade practices ranging from EC subsidization of canned fruit to Japanese quotas on leather and leather footwear.

One of the most notable section 301 investigations during the Reagan presidency involved Brazil's policy of barring imports of computer products to protect its domestic industry from foreign competition. The investigation of Brazil's computer and computer-related products policies began on September 16, 1985. On October 6, 1986, President Reagan found Brazil's policies to be an unreasonable burden and restriction on U.S. commerce. In response to Brazil's recalcitrance in opening this market, the United States prepared to retaliate but suspended the retaliation order while bilateral negotiations proceeded. The dispute was resolved.

Similarly, a section 301 investigation focused on South Korea's restrictions on beef imports and foreign insurance companies and its failure to protect intellectual property. After bilateral consultation, agreements were reached concerning the insurance markets and the intellectual property issues. The United States initiated a successful GATT dispute panel concerning the Korean beef import restrictions.

Taiwanese import restrictions regarding wine, beer, and tobacco products also drew the attention of a section 301 investigation. When Taiwan agreed to open its markets and increase access of U.S. exports of beer, wine, and cigarettes within six to twelve months, however, retaliation was suspended. President Reagan subsequently found that Taiwan was not complying with the agreement and directed the USTR to retaliate. Taiwan finally agreed to settle the dispute, and the investigation finally terminated.

The Reagan administration also initiated several section 301 investigations against what was then the European Community. On May 15, 1986, President Reagan imposed quotas on EC imports and a 200 percent tariff on a host of EC agricultural products in response to Portuguese import restrictions and Spanish tariffs. After rounds of counterretaliation, the EC and the United States settled. The EC granted tariff concessions to the United States as compensation for the Spanish and Portuguese restrictions.

Another section 301 investigation focused on EC preferential tariffs on citrus products. After determining that EC practices impaired or nullified GATT benefits, the United States imposed retaliatory tariffs of 25–40 percent on EC pasta products. The EC counterretaliated with tariffs on lemons and walnuts. The EC and the United States resolved the dispute through a series of bilateral trade concessions.

During the final year of the Reagan administration, the EC and the United States once again moved to the brink of trade war after the USTR investigated an EC ban on imports of hormone-treated beef. EC directive 146/88[24] banned the sale of hormone-treated meats regardless of origin. The measure had the goal of protecting the health of EC citizens and was not discriminatory. The United States, however, declined to submit to a GATT dispute panel on the health and technical issue. In January 1989, the USTR imposed 100 percent tariffs on EC exports of pasta, Italian juices, tomato paste, pork products, tomato sauce, and other goods in retaliation.[25] The EC threatened to impose similar tariff sanctions on U.S. exports of walnuts and dried fruits.[26]

Past administrations have found limitations in the use of section 301. President Reagan, for example, felt that the political pressures applied under section 301 might make a foreign government appear vulnerable to U.S. threats and thereby weaken its national pride. The Reagan administration felt that section 301 investigations and sanctions would work best for trade issues or sectors with little political or economic significance to the foreign government in question.

Super 301

Super 301 was an often-assailed section of the Omnibus Trade and Competitiveness Act of 1988. Under this statute, the USTR reported annually the extent to which foreign trading practices closed markets to U.S. goods or services or otherwise distorted trade. The USTR then targeted specific countries and practices for investigation and negotiation. In the event that the negotiations failed to remove the barriers on schedule, the USTR was required to impose retaliatory tariffs or quotas. The president could exercise discretion and decline to impose trade sanctions even if negotiations failed. Although the "mandatory" requirement of unilateral action is illusory under Super 301, this provision focuses such intense scrutiny on particular foreign trade practices that trade politics often require action be taken. Supporters of Super 301 believe that the threat of being named as a target will pry concessions from offending states.

When Super 301 expired in 1990, our trading partners breathed a sigh of relief as the school bully left town. Unfortunately, this relief was short-lived. In his 1992 presidential campaign platform, then candidate Bill Clinton expressed support for "a stronger, sharper Super 301." President Clinton reinstated Super 301 for two years by executive order on March 3, 1994.

Special 301

Special 301 is yet another version of section 301. Special 301, included in the 1988 Omnibus Trade and Competitiveness Act, is designed to address problems of inadequate protection of U.S. intellectual property and market access.

The USTR is mandated to identify annually by April 30 foreign states that "deny adequate and effective protection of intellectual property rights" or "deny fair and equitable market access to United States persons that rely upon intellectual property protection."

In this report to Congress, the USTR identifies countries based on the egregiousness of their offenses. Usually, this is measured in terms of damage to U.S. firms by these practices, state-sanctioned piracy of intellectual property, or the failure of these states to enter "into good faith negotiations or mak[e] significant progress in bilateral or multilateral negotiations."

The worst offenders are designated as priority foreign countries. A country in this category faces investigation by the USTR if progress at removing the offending practice is not reached in a relatively short time. In April 1994, for example, the USTR identified Argentina, India, and China as potential priority foreign countries and gave a deadline of June 30, 1994, for them to avoid investigation by the USTR.

Other categories under Special 301 include a priority watch list and a watch list. These designations signal the nations in question that the USTR is concerned with their protection of intellectual property. Countries are aware that this is generally the initial step before graduating to the priority country list. The priority watch list is usually longer than the priority list and may contain five or six countries. The watch list can be quite extensive and include eighteen or twenty countries.

Special 301 also has a special mention category. Inclusion in this category signals that although a country may "have made progress in improving their level of intellectual property protection," the "USTR believes they still need to be monitored." In other words, labeling as special mention is a way of signaling to countries that the USTR has not forgotten about them and is still watching their conduct regarding intellectual property. Special mention countries also include "countries in which problems with intellectual property protection [are] beginning to become more serious." In 1994, the USTR cited Brazil, Canada, Germany, Honduras, Israel, Panama, Paraguay, Russia, and Singapore as meriting special mention.

A country may escape from the priority list at any time at the discretion of the USTR. The USTR typically has six months after the investigation of a priority foreign country to make a determination. If the nation has made substantial progress in protecting intellectual property or if the investigation is complicated, the USTR may take nine months to make a determination.

One reason that countries may receive so much time despite prior warnings is the legislative problem of crafting an effective intellectual property regime. Before imposing sanctions on a newly industrializing state, the USTR wants to give that country every opportunity to become a responsible member of the global economic community.

Countries are selected for Special 301 designation through a variety of means. Through an annual notice placed in the *Federal Register*, the USTR requests public comment regarding countries that may be deficient in protecting intellectual property. The USTR reports that this method generates about twenty submissions a year from U.S. industry. Additional information is supplied by the U.S. Patent and Trademark Office, the U.S. Copyright Office, and the Interagency Trade Policy Staff Committee, an interagency committee composed of representatives of sixteen government agencies.

The Japanese Aftermarket for Replacement Parts

The Investigation. Since Commodore Perry and his gunboats opened Japan's markets to the United States in 1845, U.S.-Japan trade relations have been tense. The section 301 process has most frequently targeted Japanese business and trade practices. The Japanese engage in a number of restrictive trade practices. In the USTR's 1989 *National Trade Estimate: Report on Foreign Trade Barriers*, a full seventeen pages were devoted to highlighting unfair Japanese trade practices.[27] Some of the trade practices in question included legitimate concerns, such as the Japanese policy of excluding rice imports,[28] failures to protect intellectual property, and restrictions on foreign direct investment.[29] Yet the sheer volume of attention dedicated to Japanese trade practices indicated that many complaints were mere nitpicking. Section 301 investigations regarding everything from Japanese retail store requirements to import discrimination against U.S. racehorses have been proposed.

On October 1, 1994, Trade Representative Mickey Kantor initiated an investigation under section 301 of the 1974 Trade Act "with respect to certain acts, policies and practices of the Government of Japan that restrict or deny U.S. auto parts suppliers' access to the auto parts replacement and accessories market ('after-market') in Japan."

The goal of the section 301 investigation was to ascertain whether "specific barriers to access to the after-market for auto parts in Japan are unreasonable or discriminatory and burden or restrict U.S. commerce." According to the USTR, the Japanese Ministry of Transportation (MOT) regulations concerning critical parts and "alteration regulations as well as the certification system for garages and mechanics are vague and very broad in scope." Further, "they support and work in combination with market restrictive practices by Japanese auto companies and parts distributors substantially to limit foreign access to the Japanese auto parts after-market, particularly for foreign parts suppliers unable to sell original equipment to Japanese auto manufacturers." The USTR asserted that "U.S. parts suppliers could significantly expand sales to the Japanese after-market if the critical parts and alteration regulations were made clearer and less restrictive."

"The USTR requested consultations with the Government of Japan concerning the issues under investigation." A decision regarding the practices under investigation must be made within twelve months after the investigation's initiation.

Nature of the Dispute. Kantor estimated that the Japanese auto parts market drew $130 billion annually. U.S. auto parts makers had less than 2 percent of this lucrative market. According to the *National Trade Estimate: Report on Foreign Trade Barriers,* the U.S. auto parts producers lost several billion dollars annually because of restrictions in this market. A Department of Commerce study of the Japanese auto parts aftermarket determined that safety regulations pertaining to the licensing of garages and repairs denied market access to international parts producers.

Japanese auto makers traditionally purchase original equipment as manufacturer parts from members of their *keiretsu,* or formal business association. American producers have asserted that because the parts are initially designed by the supplier and not the purchasing auto maker, selection to compete for specific contracts is difficult unless producers are initially selected as the designer. Complaints also assert that the *keiretsu* system, with its financial, corporate, technical, and personnel ties, effectively excludes outsiders from competition.

Japanese auto makers and their original equipment suppliers control the aftermarket for auto parts. The USTR estimated that Japanese original equipment suppliers control over 80 percent of the aftermarket and that this market share was increasing. Most Japanese car owners service their cars at dealerships because of a strict periodic inspection schedule (known as the *shaiken*) and anxiety of failing inspection. These dealerships are unlikely to use U.S. parts. A comparison of six automobile-producing countries reveals that Japan has by far the lowest market penetration by foreign auto parts manufacturers.

Other restrictions in Japan also close the market for U.S. auto parts and stymie the establishment of a competitive parts aftermarket. The Japanese Ministry of Transportation requires that replacement of parts essential to the safety of the vehicle be made at a garage certified by the MOT. Repairs made at noncertified garages require MOT inspections.

Secrecy is another focus of U.S. complaints. According to USTR Mickey Kantor:

> The fact is, they have something called a critical parts list, I use it for an example. That list is not published anywhere. You can't

find it. But yet, you can't buy an auto part in a certified auto mechanic's shop, put in by a certified auto mechanic in Japan, if it's not on the critical parts list. It took Monroe Shock Absorbers 20 years to get the most competitive shock absorber in the world on that list. There are very few foreign competitive products on the so-called list. The labyrinth of regulations and the opaque nature of the bureaucracy and how it operates have kept foreign products out.[30]

Negotiations under Threat of Section 301. The Japanese auto industry has made some conciliatory noises regarding the auto parts dispute. On February 23, 1994, Yutaka Kume, chairman of the Japan Automobile Manufacturers Association, revealed that Japanese auto makers were considering the creation of a voluntary plan to increase purchases of imports of U.S.-made autos and auto parts. Two days later, the Nihon Keizai Shimbun announced that Toyota Motor Corporation and Nissan Motor Company had "prepared voluntary benchmarks for purchasing U.S.-made auto parts for fiscal 1995, which starts April 1, 1995." While dismissing the reports as "premature," both auto makers admitted to creating "internal purchase targets" for U.S. auto parts.

The United States, however, expressed dissatisfaction with these proposed private-sector voluntary agreements. USTR Kantor stated that such a voluntary arrangement between private-sector firms would not

> address some of the influence, as well as the barriers, that have been implemented by the Japanese government . . . which have had a negative effect on our ability to sell both auto parts and automobiles in Japan or auto parts [here] in this country to Japanese so-called transplant companies.

Herein lies an essential problem. Contrary to popular belief, the Japanese government does not have control over the auto parts or auto industry. The U.S. Department of Commerce is requesting that the Japanese auto industry "step up to the plate" and operate as U.S. companies do, "in an open, competitive way." The United States may have overestimated the degree to which the Japanese government can influence multinationals.

The United States sought an independent and neutral body to measure and gauge market penetration of U.S. auto parts in Japan. The United States also demanded the utilization of certified public accounting firms to calculate and assess market penetration. The proposed bilateral monitoring organization would comprise both American and Japanese auto industry experts.

U.S. negotiators proposed a range of quantitative indicators during talks held June 10–11, 1994. The indicators included the foreign auto sales, number of dual franchises in Japan, purchases of foreign-made auto parts by Japanese car manufacturers in Japan and overseas, purchases of U.S.-produced auto parts by Japanese auto makers in the United States, the degree of involvement by auto parts producers in the designing of Japanese cars, and market penetration by foreign auto parts makers in the Japanese aftermarket.

The Japanese proposed their own set of indicators, including the presence of foreign auto parts producer research and development facilities in Japan, the degree to which imported cars were competitively priced, the number of U.S.-made automobiles with right-side steering wheels, the visits by American auto parts makers to Japanese buyers, the number of Japanese-speaking American auto maker sales representatives working at foreign dealerships, the degree of American producer advertising for foreign-made aftermarket parts, vehicle export volumes, and collapsible rearview mirrors on foreign vehicles.

The two parties met throughout June and July 1994 but failed to agree on the objective criteria for measuring progress in opening Japan's markets. By late September 1994, the United States began to focus on Japanese nontariff barriers regarding safety and inspection in Japan. The Japanese Ministry of International Trade and Investment was reportedly willing to grant some of these concessions. The areas of regulation, however, were subject not to MITI's control, but to the jurisdiction of the Ministry of Transportation. The MOT acquiesced in one small sector by removing certain shock absorbers from the list of important safety parts. This move opened a small sector of the market for U.S. auto parts makers.

But the Japanese government vigorously objected to the U.S. demand for extensive and wholesale deregulation of the auto parts aftermarket. Minister of International Trade and Industry Ryutaro Hashimoto asserted that the goal of the section 301 investigation was an end to a regulatory system that was crucial to automotive safety in Japan. U.S. Ambassador to Japan Walter Mondale responded that the United States had no objection to regulations truly designed to promote public safety and prevent accidents. Mondale maintained that the true issue involved the use of safety-related rules as a protectionist method to close the auto parts aftermarket.

Mr. Hashimoto of MITI announced that Japan remained amenable to discussing the "maximum possible deregulation without damaging safety." A major problem was the Japanese belief that all their auto parts regulations were essential to maintain public safety. Accordingly, the MITI negotiators offered a plan of "deregulation to be considered auto part by auto part, and then, only in response to foreign petitions." The USTR objected, complaining that the petition procedure was vague and did not constitute "a credible form of deregulation."[31]

The U.S. auto part makers generally supported the administration's section 301 action against Japan. As Lee Kadrich, director of government affairs and international trade for the Automotive Parts and Accessories Association, noted, however, "Japan's after market for parts is the smallest of four Japanese parts markets. Japan's domestic market for original equipment, the market for original equipment of Japanese transplant automakers in the U.S., and the after market for Japanese cars in the United States are all bigger slices of the economic pie."[32]

Settlement of the U.S.-Japan Auto Parts Dispute

In late June 1995, the United States and Japan reached an agreement in the auto parts sector. Under the agreement, the Japanese agreed to deregulate the auto parts market and increase the amount of domestic content used in cars produced domestically by Japanese auto makers.

Japanese auto makers also pledged to increase production of cars made in the United States that used U.S.-made parts. The Japanese, however, had been steadily increasing their purchases of U.S. auto parts, from $2.5 billion in 1986 to nearly $20 billion in 1994. These purchases were parts of commitments that did not guarantee set purchasers although the USTR seemed to interpret these commitments as guarantees. Indeed, this interpretation largely explains Japanese reluctance to embrace further "voluntary" targets in the future.

Another part of the agreement addresses U.S. access to auto dealerships in Japan. The agreement calls for MITI to send letters to Japanese auto dealerships saying that they are free to carry any brands and that indications otherwise by Japanese car dealers could violate national monopoly laws.

The Japanese also agreed to deregulate some of the parts from their critical parts list. Certain struts, shock absorbers, power steering, and trailer hitches will be opened for competition from U.S. firms.

Furthermore, the Japanese had been negotiating with the United States on how to review auto parts for inclusion. The U.S. Trade Representative advocated swifter changes while the Japanese Ministry of Transportation favored a part-by-part review. In the end, Japan agreed to a one-year review of the critical parts list. Parts not central to health and safety concerns will be deregulated.

One area of progress is in the Japanese auto inspection procedure. Under the agreement, Japan will relax the standards for garage certification. By lowering these costs, USTR Kantor predicted that 7,000 to 8,000 new repair garages would open in Japan in the next five years. Kantor said that "what this will do is create the ability for garages to carry on inspections and spread competition across Japan, which will help to break up a system which was keeping prices high and was over-charging for parts, and was making inspections and repair very difficult."

GATT Consistency and Section 301

Critics have asserted that section 301 will be scrapped in favor of the WTO dispute settlement mechanism under Article 23 of the GATT. This provision requires members of the WTO to use its dispute settlement procedures whenever they seek redress of a violation of obligations or other nullification or impairment. It also states that members shall "abide by the rules and procedures of this understanding." If the United States pursued an independent and unilateral course of retaliation while ignoring the GATT, this action would be inconsistent with Article 23.

The United States, however, is not required to submit to Article 23. During the GATT legislative debate, members of Congress were careful not to abandon their option for unilateral action. The GATT implementation legislation, H.R. 5110, provided specifically that no provision of the Uruguay Round Agreements, nor the application of any such provision to any person or circumstance that is inconsistent with any law of the United States, shall have effect. Section 301 is specifically acknowledged as being untouched by the GATT. If the United States pursued sanctions under section 301, it would face an adverse ruling from the WTO dispute settlement panel for disregarding its obligations under Article 23. This situation might result in WTO authorization of countermeasures by the other party to the dispute.

Critique of Section 301

Section 301 shifts the burden of our economy's problems and is blatantly protectionist; this violates the spirit of the GATT. But section 301 poses other problems. First and foremost, as evidenced in the hormone-treated beef dispute with the EC, clearly section 301 invites the escalation of retaliatory trade actions. Trade war mirrors the military counterpart; no one ever truly wins, and innocent civilians are injured. The civilians in these disputes are the importers, exporters, and consumers of the products facing higher tariffs in response to an unfair trade practice in a totally unrelated area of the economy. The pasta manufacturers in Italy were threatened by U.S. retaliation for actions in the EC beef industry. Arguably, trade wars are purposefully targeted at innocent civilians in the exporter states. Because the EC does not export beef to the United States, meaningful retaliation cannot be aimed at the European beef industry. Therefore, section 301 actions necessarily target parties unrelated to the dispute. But, to make the action even more powerful, the United States traditionally targets an equivalent value of exports from a vulnerable industry or state. Thus, in the EC-hormone case, the Italian exports of pasta and tomato products were targeted because the Italian economy is more fragile than the economies of the United Kingdom, Germany, France, and the Netherlands. To return to the military analogy, the United States is retaliating against an attack on a naval base by bombing a foreign orphanage.

It is questionable whether section 301 is a proper tool of trade policy. Section 301 is contrary to GATT principles of nondiscrimination and MFN treatment.[33] If the United States turns its back on the multilateral dispute mechanisms of the GATT, it exposes itself to similar attacks from our trading partners. Fifty-one countries joined in a GATT council meeting condemning the use of section 301 as violative of the GATT in January 1989.[34] U.S. actions that discriminate against or restrict foreign investment may be the fuel for a "foreign-designed section 301 action" by our trading partners.

The discriminatory methods of addressing patent infringement and other intellectual property disputes under section 337 (discussed earlier) might similarly provide our partners with grounds for unilateral sanctions. Many prominent trade economists such as Jagdish Bhagwati have asserted that countries such as Japan should develop their own section 301 legislation as a counter to our unilateral actions. To date, we are indeed fortunate that our trading partners have elected to seek resolution of these problems in the GATT instead of imitating our strategies in section 301.

APPENDIX

Agencies in International Trade

Department of Commerce

The Department of Commerce is the largest federal agency involved with international trade. The department is headed by the secretary of commerce. Its international trade functions include promoting American exports, investigating allegations of unfair foreign trade practices, and licensing U.S. exports. The following divisions of the Department of Commerce are most significant in international trade.

International Trade Administration. Directed by the under secretary of commerce for international trade, the International Trade Administration was established in 1980. The express purpose of ITA is to strengthen the international trade and investment position of the United States. ITA is responsible for import administration, trade development, and nonagricultural trade operations of the U.S. government. ITA also supports the trade policy negotiation efforts of the U.S. trade representative.

ITA administers the investigative aspects of the antidumping and countervailing duty laws, as well as various trade arrangements. Two assistant secretaries report to the under secretary. The assistant secretary for import administration administers antidumping and countervailing duty laws. The assistant secretary for international economic policy oversees the country desks of the department and monitors bilateral, multilateral, and regional economic policy.[1] Another part of ITA is the U.S. and Foreign Commercial Service. The USFCS provides international marketing assistance to U.S. producers. USFCS has 68 offices throughout the United States and 132 offices in sixty-eight countries. It also conducts specific market research and promotes American exports through trade fairs, exhibitions, trade missions, and overseas trade seminars.

ITA develops international trade and investment policies on specific industries, acts as a liaison between industries and the federal government, and provides support for sectoral aspects of the

119

multilateral trade negotiations through seventeen industry-sector advisory committees. ITA promotes the formation of export trading companies and issues certificates of review providing them with limited exemption from liability under the antitrust laws.

Bureau of Export Administration. Headed by the under secretary of commerce for export administration, the Bureau of Export Administration is responsible for implementing much of U.S. export control policy. BXA activities include export licensing, research on relaxation of export controls, and enforcement of export control laws. Two assistant secretaries report to the under secretary. The assistant secretary for export administration oversees export licensing, foreign availability studies, and nonproliferation issues. The assistant secretary for export enforcement investigates violations of export controls and administers the antiboycott provisions of the Export Administration Act.[2]

Department of State

The Department of State is responsible for general coordination and supervision of U.S. foreign relations and is the lead agency for all interdepartmental activity in international affairs. The under secretary for economic and agricultural affairs is the principal adviser to the secretary on foreign economic policy, including international trade, agriculture, energy, finance, transportation, and relations with developing countries. The assistant secretary for economic and business affairs is responsible for foreign economic policy, including resource and food policy, international energy issues, trade and trade controls, international finance and development, aviation, maritime affairs, and the Arms and Munitions Control Act. The Department of State recently established an Office of Business Affairs to assist corporations operating overseas.

Department of the Treasury

The Treasury Department is responsible for formulating U.S. domestic and international financial, economic, and tax policy. The secretary of the Treasury serves as the U.S. governor on the International Monetary Fund as well as other international development banks.[3] The under secretary for international affairs is the principal adviser to the secretary on international economic policy, including international monetary affairs, trade and investment policy, international debt strategy, and participation in international financial institutions. The assistant secretary for international affairs reports to the under secretary for international affairs on international monetary, financial, commercial, energy, and trade matters and is also responsible for financial diplomacy, international monetary system operations, foreign exchange markets, participation in the IMF and multilateral development banks, foreign investments in the United States, and U.S. investments abroad. The department also has a substantial presence in international trade by its administration of the Customs Service.

Customs Service. Established by the first Congress in 1789,[4] the Customs Service became an agency within the Treasury Department in 1927.[5] Responsible for collecting tariffs and enforcing customs laws,[6] Customs is the principal border enforcement agency. The Customs Service seizes contraband and processes persons, carriers, cargo, and mail into and out of the United States. The Customs Service also enforces export control laws and intercepts illegal high-technology exports. Providing information to importers and exporters regarding international trade is another function of the Customs Service.

The Customs Service is headed by the commissioner of customs. There are 240 customs ports and stations. Approximately a dozen Customs offices are abroad.

Office of the U.S. Trade Representative

The first U.S. trade representative (USTR), formerly called the special trade representative, was appointed by President John Kennedy in 1963.[7] The USTR is responsible for directing all trade negotiations and formulating all trade policy for the United States. This office is the chief representative to the World Trade Organization (WTO), the Organization for Economic Cooperation and Development (OECD), and the United Nations Conference on Trade and Development. The Office of the USTR became an agency of the Executive Office of the President in 1974.[8] It is one of the smallest agencies engaged in international trade. The USTR is assisted by three deputies and several assistants, each primarily responsible for trade in a particular region or representing the United States at the WTO.

International Trade Commission

Originally called the Tariff Commission, the International Trade Commission is an independent agency that investigates antidumping and countervailing duty issues and determines whether a domestic industry is materially injured (or so threatened) by imports sold at less than fair value (dumped) or subsidized by a foreign government.[9] Injuries to domestic industries from rapidly rising imports from nonmarket economies and fairly traded imports are also investigated by the ITC. Additionally, the ITC investigates allegations of unfair patent, trademark, or copyright import practices.[10]

The ITC also operates as a research arm of Congress and the executive branch, producing studies, reports, and recommendations involving international trade and tariffs to the president,[11] Congress,[12] and government agencies.[13] The ITC has broad power to investigate compliance with customs laws, the volume of importation in comparison with domestic production and consumption, and all matters relating to competition between foreign and U.S. industries.

The ITC is composed of six commissioners appointed by the president and confirmed by the Senate for nine-year terms, with the chairman and the vice chairman appointed by the president for two-year terms. No more than three commissioners may be of the same political party. The chairman and the vice chairman are appointed from the existing commissioners by the president but may not be the two most recently appointed commissioners.

Export-Import Bank

The Export-Import Bank is an independent federal agency[14] responsible for promoting American exports through loans, loan guarantees, and grants. While generally directed at matching foreign government subsidies, under some circumstances the Exim Bank subsidizes American exports without any foreign subsidized competitor.[15] The Exim Bank is not to compete with private financing but rather to supplement the private sector.

The Exim Bank acts to reduce the risks of buyer default for American exporters under a variety of insurance programs. Its policies insure against risks of default in export transactions and are available in a variety of insurance plans that are tailored to the special needs of different types of exporters and financial institutions.

Other Exim Bank programs include the Working Capital Guarantee Program, a loan guarantee program designed to provide eligible exporters with access to working capital loans from commercial lenders, and the Engineering Multiplier Program, which provides financing in support of project-related design services or feasibility studies with potential for generating further procurement of American exports.

Overseas Private Investment Corporation

The Overseas Private Investment Corporation was established to encourage U.S. private investment in developing countries to promote social and economic development, increase U.S. jobs and exports, serve as an alternative to government-to-government lending, and promote private sector economies in developing countries. OPIC offers investors political risk insurance, loan guarantees, and direct loans. It also provides investors assistance in finding investment opportunities. Currently, OPIC is involved in projects in over 100 developing countries.

The political risks against which OPIC insures include expropriation, inconvertibility of local currency holdings, damage from war, revolution, insurrection, or civil strife, and arbitrary drawings of letters of credit. The corporation guarantees payment of principal and interest on loans up to $50 million. Direct Investment Fund loans range from $500,000 to $6 million, for terms of seven to twelve years, with interest rates based on project risk. These loans and loan guarantees are limited to facility creation, expansion or modernization, or new inputs of technology or services that in turn encourage new investment.

OPIC also offers preinvestment services, including the Investor Information Service, an investment data clearinghouse; the Opportunity Bank, a computerized investor-project matching service, and the Investment Missions Programs, which provides senior U.S. business executives the opportunity to discuss investment possibilities with host country officials and businesses.

OPIC is an independent federal agency affiliated with the Agency for International Development[16] and is governed by a board of fifteen directors, eight from the private sector and seven from the federal government.

Trade and Development Agency

The Trade and Development Agency is an independent federal agency[17] that promotes economic development and U.S. exports in developing states. TDA funds feasibility studies by U.S. firms for projects financed by the World Bank, other international financial institutions, or host countries. Under section 607(a), TDA is the co-ordinating authorizing agency for government-to-government technical assistance. Under section 661, the agency funds planning services, feasibility studies, orientation visits, and trade-related training for U.S. firms involved in development projects with high export potential. TDA is also responsible for carrying out a program of tied aid credits for U.S. exports.

Court of International Trade

Formerly the Customs Courts, the Court of International Trade is a specialized court with jurisdiction over any civil claims arising from federal import laws.[18] Cases before the CIT typically involve customs classification and valuation issues, antidumping and countervailing duty cases, and petitions for adjustment assistance. The court consists of nine judges and one chief judge, no more than five of whom may belong to any one political party. As an Article 3 court, it functions like a federal district court and has the same broad equitable powers. There is no right to a jury trial before the CIT. Most matters are heard by one judge. If constitutional issues, executive orders, or broad customs issues are implicated, however, the chief judge may appoint a three-judge panel to hear the case. In these cases, a majority decision is required. The CIT has jurisdiction over appeals to antidumping or countervailing duty investigations between the United States and Canada if neither party requests formation of a binational panel.

The court is located in New York but may sit at any port within the jurisdiction of the United States. Appeals are taken to the U.S. Court of Appeals for the Federal Circuit, with ultimate review by the Supreme Court.

Organization for Economic Cooperation and Development

The Organization for Economic Cooperation and Development is the successor to the organization created in 1948 to implement the

Marshall Plan. OECD seeks to promote sustainable economic growth, employment, and standards of living in member countries, while contributing to the development of less developed nonmember countries. Initial membership included eighteen European countries, Canada, and the United States, with Japan, Finland, Australia, Mexico, and New Zealand joining later. The OECD has expanded its scope to address international trade standards and corporate codes of conduct.

UN Conference on Trade and Development

Initially created in 1964, UNCTAD is an organ of the UN General Assembly that examines and provides a forum for discussion on international economic and trade issues and their impact on development.

World Bank

Officially known as the International Bank for Reconstruction and Development, the World Bank is an international financial development institution created in 1945. The bank finances development projects in the third world. These projects are financed by the sale of bonds, which are repaid by the projects financed. The World Bank is located in Washington, D.C.

World International Property Organization

Often referred to as WIPO, this organization is the agency of the United Nations that deals with the global protection of intellectual property. The Berne Union (which protects copyrights and intellectual property) and the Paris Club (which protects patented goods) are both administered by WIPO.

Notes

CHAPTER 2: HISTORY OF U.S. POLICY

1. Congress's decision to reject the dumping code raised serious concerns about the future of the trading system. Foreign governments were concerned about making agreements—and paying the political price at home—if Congress ultimately rejected the president's commitments. The Nixon administration therefore proposed a deal with Congress: Congress would set the parameters of the executive's negotiating authority in advance and would consult with the executive on the preparation of implementing legislation. Such legislation would be subject to an up-or-down vote by both houses of Congress within a set time frame, with no amendments. This fast-track procedure has governed all U.S. trade negotiations since the Kennedy Round.

2. Section 301 of the Trade Act of 1974 provides for retaliatory actions against foreign states that unjustifiably burden or restrict U.S. commerce or deny U.S. rights under international trade agreements.

3. *U.S.Code Supp.*, vol. 19, sec. 3512 (a)2(b)(1995).

4. NAFTA Renegotiation and WTO Dispute Settlement Review Commission Act, H.R. 78, 105th Cong., 1st sess., 1997.

CHAPTER 3: ANTIDUMPING

1. *Smith-Corona Group v. United States,* 713 F.2d 1568, 1575 (Fed. Cir. 1983).

2. *American Permac, Inc. v. United States,* 703 F. Supp. 97, 100–101 (Ct. Int'l Trade 1988).

3. The Commerce Department may itself initiate an investigation but does so rarely. Historically, the department has initiated an investigation only as an adjunct to an investigation initiated by a petition. In the course of a dumping case involving semiconductors with 64-kilobit dynamic random access memory from Japan, for example, the department realized that the pace of technology would quickly make any antidumping order on that product irrelevant. Commerce therefore instituted an investigation into the next generation of DRAMs, 256-kilobit chips. In light of developments in the industry and the inability of the legal mechanism to keep pace with technological developments, the United States and Japan ultimately entered into a special arrangement concerning trade in memory chips.

4. The products covered by this investigation are certain paper clips, wholly of wire base metal, whether or not galvanized, whether or not plated with nickel or other base metal (for example, copper), with a wire diameter between 0.025 inches and 0.075 inches regardless of physical configuration, except as specifically excluded. The products subject to this investigation

include but are not limited to clips commercially referred to as No. 1 clips, No. 3 clips, Jumbo or Giant Clips, Gem Clips, Frictioned Clips, Perfect Gems, Marcel Gems, Universal Clips, Nifty Clips, Peerless Clips, Ring Clips, and Glide-on Clips.

Specifically excluded from the scope of this investigation are plastic and vinyl-covered paper clips, butterfly clips, or other paper fasteners that are not made wholly of wire base metal. See *Federal Register* 59, October 7, 1994: 51,168, 51,169.

5. *Koyo Seiko Co., Ltd. v. United States,* 36 F.3d 1565, 1568 (Fed. Cir. 1994).

6. For these purposes, unless otherwise noted, the reference to injury or injured includes the threat of material injury to or material retardation of the establishment of a domestic industry.

7. 132 F.3d 716 (Fed. Cir. 1997).

8. Ibid.

Chapter 4: Countervailing Duties

1. For an early ITC discussion of CADIC analysis, see *3.5" Microdisks and Media Therefor from Japan*, Inv. 731-TA-389 (Preliminary), USITC Pub. 2076 (Additional Views of Commissioner Cass) (Washington, D.C.: USITC, 1988).

Chapter 5: Escape Clause

1. *U.S. Code,* vol. 19, sec. 2251 et seq.

2. Ibid., sec. 2252(h)(1).

3. See H.R. Rep. 576, 100th Cong., 2d sess., 1988: 663–64.

4. *U.S. Code,* vol. 19, sec. 2252(a)(5).

5. Ibid., sec. 2252(b)(2)(B).

6. Ibid., sec. 2252(b)(4).

7. *Apple Juice,* Inv. TA-201-59, USITC Pub. 1861 (Washington, D.C., 1986).

8. *Heavyweight Motorcycles,* Inv. TA-201-47, USITC Pub. 1342 (Washington, D.C.: USITC, 1983).

9. *Certain Metal Castings,* Inv. TA-201-58, USITC Pub. 1849 (Washington, D.C.: USITC, 1986).

10. *Certain Knives,* Inv. TA-201-61, USITC Pub. 2107 (Washington, D.C.: USITC, 1988).

11. S. Rep. 1298, 93d Cong., 2d sess. 1974: 119.

12. See, for example, *Electric Shavers and Parts Thereof,* Inv. TA-201-57, USITC Pub. 1819 (Washington, D.C.: USITC, 1986).

13. *U.S. Code,* vol. 19, sec. 2252(c)(1)(A)(i).

14. Ibid., sec. 2252(c)(B).

15. Ibid., sec. 252(b)(1)(B).

16. *Wood Shakes and Shingles,* Inv. TA-201-56 (Washington, D.C.: USITC, 1976).

17. *U.S. Code,* vol. 19, sec. 2252(e)(1) et seq.

18. ITC General Counsel Memorandum GC-I-101 (Washington, D.C.: USITC, June 4, 1985).

19. *U.S. Code,* vol. 19, sec. 2252(b)(3)(B).

20. Amendment 1022 to Amendment 1015 to H.R. 1562, *Congressional Record,* 131st Cong., 1st sess., 1985: 5582.

21. The four-year period of relief was "to provide time for the industry to complete important investment projects, improve productivity, and regain profitability." Ronald Reagan, "Letter to the Speaker of the House and the President of the Senate on Import Relief for the Specialty Steel Industry," *Public Papers of the Presidents of the United States: Ronald Reagan, 1983,* vol. 2 (Washington, D.C.: Government Printing Office, 1985), pp. 1016–17.

CHAPTER 6: NONMARKET ECONOMIES

1. See, generally, *Discussion of Statutory Criteria under Section 406 of the Trade Act,* USITC General Counsel Memorandum (Washington, D.C.: USITC, May 9, 1986).

2. *Honey from China,* USITC Pub. TA-406-13 (Washington, D.C.: USITC, 1994).

3. William J. Clinton, "Message to the Congress Reporting on Trade with China," *Public Papers of the Presidents of the United States: William J. Clinton, 1994,* vol. 1 (Washington, D.C.: Government Printing Office, 1995), p. 747.

4. *Ammonium Paratungstate and Tungstic Acid from the People's Republic of China,* USITC Pub. TA-406-11 (Washington, D.C.: USITC, 1987).

5. Ibid.

6. Ibid.

7. "Implementation of an Orderly Marketing Agreement on Ammonium Paratungstate and Tungstic Acid," *Federal Register,* vol. 52, no. 37 (1987): 275

8. *Federal Register,* vol. 52 (1987): 37,275.

9. *Anhydrous Ammonia from the U.S.S.R.,* USITC Pub. TA-406-5 (Washington, D.C.: USITC, 1979).

10. Spencer Rich, "Soviets Dumping Ammonia, ITC Says," *Washington Post,* Oct. 4, 1979.

11. *Anhydrous Ammonia,* USITC, p. 5.

12. Ibid.

13. Ibid.

14. *Anhydrous Ammonia from the U.S.S.R.,* USITC Pub. TA-406-6 (Washington, D. C.: USITC, 1980).

15. "Clothespins, Report to the President," *Federal Register,* vol. 46 (1981): 62,338

16. *Oscillating Fans from China,* USITC Pub. TA-406-12 (Washington, D.C.: USITC, June 10, 1992).

17. Ibid.

18. *Ferrosilicon from the Union of Soviet Socialist Republics,* Inv. TA-406-10 (Washington, D.C.: USITC, 1984).

19. *Canned Mushrooms from the People's Republic of China,* USITC Pub.1293, TA-406-9 (Washington, D.C.: USITC, 1982).

20. See *Legal Issues in Canned Mushrooms from the People's Republic of China,* USITC Pub., General Counsel Memorandum (Washington, D.C.: USITC, September 17, 1982).

CHAPTER 7: NATIONAL SECURITY

1. *U.S. Code,* vol. 19, sec. 2862.

2. George Bush, "Presidential Decision," *Federal Register,* vol. 54 (April 3, 1989): 13,397.

3. Ibid.

4. George Bush, "Presidential Decision," *Federal Register,* vol. 54 (November 9, 1989): 47,099.

5. Ibid.

6. *Daily Report for Executives (BNA): Regulation, Economics, and Law,* DER 205, October 25, 1989, p. A-7.

7. Ronald Reagan, "Presidential Decision," *Federal Register,* vol. 54 (January 18, 1989): 1,974.

8. Ibid.

9. *Federal Contracts Report (BNA),* 50 DER 22, December 5, 1988, p. 918.

10. Ibid.

11. "U.S. Ceramic Package Industry Weak, but Could Be Revived," *International Trade Report (BNA),* 10 DER 48, December 8, 1993, p. 2,046; "Report of Disposition of Section 232 National Security Import Investigation of Ceramic Semiconductor Packages," *Federal Register,* vol. 58 (September 14, 1993): 48,033.

12. "Report of Ceramic Semiconductor Packages."

13. Ibid.

14. "Inside BXA," *Export Control News,* vol. 7, no. 8 (August 26, 1993).

15. Ronald Reagan, "Message to the Congress Reporting on Petroleum Imports and Energy Security," *Public Papers of the Presidents of the United States: Ronald Regan, 1988–1989,* vol. 2 (Washington, D.C.: Government Printing Office, 1991), pp. 1,675–76.

16. President Reagan announced his decision just a few weeks before the end of his presidency. Some believe this allowed President Reagan to avoid having to take action to stem imports. Ibid.

17. "Commerce Denies Petition to Adjust Oil Imports Saying It Would Violate the Law," *BNA Management Briefing,* January 26, 1994.

18. "Commerce Department Explores Oil Imports Security Threat," *Octane Week,* vol. 9, no. 24 (June 13, 1994).

19. "U.S. Security Threat from Oil Imports at Issue," *Oil and Gas Journal,* vol. 92, no. 25 (June 20, 1994): 25.

20. Ibid.

21. Ibid.

22. Ibid.

23. "Machine Tool Makers Say Japanese Imports Threaten National Security, Ask for Curbs," *International Trade Report (BNA),* vol. 8, no. 11 (June 15, 1983): 426.

24. "President Says U.S. Will Seek Machine Tool Restraints, National Security Ruling Delayed," *International Trade Report,* vol. 3, no. 22 (May 28, 1986): 711.

25. "Machine Tool Case Gains Renewed White House Attention as Congressional Pressures Grow," *International Trade Report,* vol. 3, no. 6 (February 5, 1986): 181.

26. Ronald Reagan, "Statement on the Machine Tool Industry," *Public Papers of the Presidents of the United States: Ronald Reagan, 1986,* vol. 1 (Washington, D.C.: Government Printing Office, 1988), pp. 632–33.

27. Clyde H. Farnsworth, "Reagan Acts to Restrict Machine Tool Imports," *New York Times,* May 21, 1986, p. D-1.

<h2 style="text-align:center">CHAPTER 8: INTELLECTUAL PROPERTY</h2>

1. *U.S. Code,* vol. 19, sec. 1337.

2. *Certain Automatic Crankspin Grinders,* Inv. 337-TA-60, USITC Pub. 1022 (Washington, D.C.: USITC, 1979).

3. *Certain Inclined-Field Acceleration Tubes, Inc.,* Inv. 337-TA-67 (Washington, D.C.: USITC, 1980).

4. While the ITC and some courts have referred to a section 337 investigation as in rem, this is not precisely correct. An in rem action involves the status of a particular piece of property and is often seen in cases involving government confiscation or questions of title. An ITC investigation is really a legislative rulemaking proceeding conducted according to adjudicative procedures. A section 337 order is similar to an administrative regulation that bars the importation of all goods—not a particular piece of property—that meet certain specifications.

<h2 style="text-align:center">CHAPTER 9: TRADE RETALIATION</h2>

1. *U.S. Code,* vol. 19, sec. 2411 et seq.

2. Ibid., sec. 2411(a)(1)(B)(ii).

3. Ibid., sec. 2411(c)(1)(A).

4. Ibid., sec. 2411(c)(1)(C).

5. Ibid., sec. 2411(b)(4)(A).

6. Ibid., sec. 2411(d)(3)(A).

7. Ibid., sec. 2411(d)(3)(D).

8. Ibid., sec. 2411(c)(1)(B).

9. Ibid., sec. 2411(a)(3)(A).

10. Ibid., sec. 2411(a)(4)(B).

11. Ibid., sec. 2411(d)(3)(B)(iii).

12. The USTR prepares that report pursuant to section 1818 of the Trade Act of 1974, as amended by section 303 of the Trade and Tariff Act of 1984 and section 1304 of the Omnibus Trade and Competitiveness Act of 1988.

13. Japan, for example, received twenty pages of attention in the 1992 U.S. Trade Representative's *National Trade Estimate: Report on Foreign Trade Barriers* (Washington, D.C.: Government Printing Office, 1992).

14. Ibid.

15. Ibid., p. 1.

16. Ibid., pp. 1–2.

17. Ibid., p. 1.

18. "No Sanctions on India Trade," *New York Times,* June 15, 1990, p. 6.

19. Karen Riley, "Bush Will Be Buddy, Not Bully to Japan," *Washington Times,* April 30, 1990, p. B5.

20. *National Trade Estimates,* p. 119.

21. K. K. Sherma, "India Attracts More Foreign Investment," *Financial Times*, February 8, 1989, p. 4.

22. "Section 301 Sanction Judged Inappropriate, World Insurance Report," *Financial Times*, June 22, 1990.

23. "India Rebuffs U.S. Trade Sanction Threat," *Los Angeles Times*, May 1, 1990, p. 5.

24. Directive 146/88, introduced January 1, 1988.

25. "USTR Yeutter Confirms U.S. Intention to Retaliate against EC Meat Hormone Ban," *BNA Daily Report for Executives*, December 28, 1988.

26. "U.S., EEC Officials Meet over Farm Subsidy Disagreements," *Los Angeles Times*, March 11, 1989, p. 10; "House Panel Chairmen Consider Plan to Block Sale of EC Food Products to U.S. Military," *BNA International Trade Reporter*, March 22, 1989.

27. *National Trade Estimates*, 1989.

28. Paul Rosenthal, "A Lose-Lose Trade Bargain? How the Democrats Could Turn GATT into a Hot Campaign Issue," *Washington Post*, February 16, 1992.

29. Ibid.

30. Mickey Kantor, testimony before U.S. House Committee on Ways and Means, Subcommittee on Trade, March 15, 1994.

31. *International Trade Report*, vol. 11 (October 19, 1994): 41.

32. "Bilateral Negotiations: U.S.-Japan Reach Deal on Insurance, Procurement but Auto Talks Still Stuck," *International Trade Report*, vol. 12 (October 5, 1995).

33. General Agreement on Tariffs and Trade Article 1 provides for most-favored-nation status. GATT Article 2 of the agreement is violated if the United States unilaterally imposes higher duties on imports contrary to the GATT binding level.

34. Jagdish Bhagwati, "Big Bite Flouts the Rules," *New York Times*, June 4, 1989, p. F-2.

APPENDIX

1. Those trade policies include the U.S.-EEC arrangement and nineteen other steel trade arrangements; the machine tool arrangements with Japan and Taiwan; the U.S.-Japan semiconductor agreement; and the U.S.-Canada Memorandum of Understanding on Softwood Lumber.

2. *U.S. Code*, vol. 50, app. 2401 et seq.

3. Those banks include the International Bank for Reconstruction and Development, the Inter-American Development Bank, and the African Development Bank.

4. *U.S. Statutes at Large* 1: 24.

5. *U.S. Code*, vol. 19, sec. 2071.

6. Those laws include the Tariff Act of 1930 (*U.S. Code*, vol. 19, sec. 1654).

7. See Executive Order 11075.

8. Trade Act of 1974 (*U.S. Code*, vol. 19, sec. 2171) created that office.

9. Title 7 of the Tariff Act of 1930 and section 201 of the Trade Act of 1974 give the commission that authority.

10. Section 337 of the Tariff Act of 1930 authorizes that activity.

11. Specifically, the ITC advises the president on trade negotiations (*U.S. Code*, vol. 19, sec. 2151), GSP issues (*U.S. Code*, vol. 19, sec. 2151, 2163), section 201 "safeguard" issues (*U.S. Code*, vol. 19, sec. 2251–2254), bilateral "safeguard" issues under NAFTA (*U.S. Code*, vol. 19, sec. 3351–3356), section 301 issues relating to imports from Communist countries (*U.S. Code*, vol. 19, sec. 2436), and agricultural import issues (*U.S. Code*, vol. 7, sec. 624).

12. Specifically, the ITC reports to the House Ways and Means Committee and the Senate Finance Committee. These committees have the power to request directly that the ITC conduct studies (*U.S. Code*, vol. 19, sec. 1332).

13. The ITC, for example, cooperates with the Departments of Treasury and Commerce in establishing a uniform method of aggregating statistical data on exports and imports with domestic production data (*U.S. Code*, vol. 19, sec. 1484).

14. The Export-Import Bank Act of 1945 (*U.S. Code*, vol. 12, sec. 635) established that agency.

15. This is particularly true in cases where the export sale would be lost but for Exim Bank financing. Paradoxically, however, the buyer of the exports must be creditworthy.

16. OPIC is under the same parent organization as the Agency for International Development: the International Development Cooperation Agency. The IDCA is, however, essentially a phantom organization that the director of AID has run in an "acting" capacity since the mid-1980s. Significantly, to the extent that policy makers ever intended OPIC to be subordinate to another agency, it is not so today.

17. TDA became an independent agency in 1992 as a result of the Jobs through Exports Act, which amended sections 607(a) and 661 of the Foreign Assistance Act of 1961 (*U.S. Code*, vol. 2, sec. 2357, 2421).

18. The court actually dates back to 1890, when Congress established it as the Board of U. S. General Appraisers (*U.S. Code*, vol. 19, ch. 4). It later became the Customs Court in 1926 (*U.S. Code*, vol. 19, sec. 405a), was integrated into the court system in 1939 and 1948 (*U.S. Code*, vol. 28, sec. 1582, 1583), and became an Article 3 court in 1956 (*U.S. Code*, vol. 28, sec. 251).

Glossary

Bounty. Payment by a nation to producers to encourage exports and improve the competitive position of those producers in global markets.

Comparative Advantage. Theory of international trade law first espoused by economist David Ricardo in 1817, stating that a nation should specialize in the production and export of those goods and services that it produces more efficiently than other goods and services and import goods and services where it has a comparative disadvantage.

Countervailing Duty. Duty or tax imposed on imports to counter the advantages or market distortions of export or other subsidies provided by the exporting nation.

Drawback. The practice of refunding all or part of the import duties assessed when imported goods are reexported or used in the manufacture of exported goods.

Dumping. The sale of an imported good at less than fair value. Under U.S. law, less than fair value is a price lower than the price charged in the exporter's home market or that of third-country markets.

Embargo. A ban on the exports or imports of a particular nation or product. The United States, for example, has a trade embargo prohibiting importing or exporting most goods to Cuba. Similarly, the United States has a ban on imports of ivory and other products from endangered species.

Export Performance Requirements. Requirements of an exporting state that a producer export a certain amount of its output to receive a subsidy or other economic benefit from the government. The regulation may also require that a specific amount of domestic content be included in the product for export.

Export Restraints. Often referred to as orderly marketing arrangements or voluntary restraint agreements. These are restrictions by exporting states to limit the amount of exports to a given foreign market. These restrictions are typically established by the exporting nation as a concession to the importing nation to avoid more draconian solutions.

Foreign Trade Zone. Program under which goods may be imported into designated areas of the United States free of duties. In a foreign trade zone, imported goods have value added in the United States and are then either exported or imported into the United States with no tariff on the value added within the foreign trade zone.

Free Trade Area or Free Trade Agreement. A group of two or more nations or customs territories in which tariffs and other trade restrictions are eliminated on substantially all intragroup trade in products originating in member nations. Examples of free trade areas are the North American Free Trade Agreement (NAFTA) and the South American Common Market, Mercado Común del Sur (MERCOSUR).

Generalized System of Preferences. Preferential trade program of the United States under which imports from developing states may enter under a lower tariff or free from tariffs.

Harmonized Tariff Schedule of the United States. Comprehensive directory of tariff classifications and rates of goods that enter customs.

Intellectual Property. Property right based on patents, trademarks, and copyrights.

Less than Fair Value. See *Dumping*.

Most-Favored-Nation Treatment. Fundamental principle of the World Trade Organization that requires that all member nations afford the same tariff treatment given to most-favored nations. Pursuant to GATT Article 1, the contracting parties agree to extend most-favored-nation status to each other. Under U.S. trade policy, the doctrine of most-favored-nation treatment may be traced to early friend-ship, commerce, and navigation treaties of 1778.

Multilateral Agreement. An international agreement that involves three or more nations as parties. Examples are the World Trade Organization and NAFTA.

National Treatment. International trade principle that requires that a nation accord to goods of a producer from another nation treatment no less favorable than the most favorable treatment that the nation accords to domestic producers. National treatment requires nations not to discriminate against goods or capital from another nation after those goods have cleared customs. It prohibits a nation from granting preferential treatment to domestic firms owned by its nationals as opposed to domestic firms controlled by foreign investors.

Nonmarket Economy. A country in which the government engages in central economic planning and largely controls economic activity. This is in contrast to market economies, where market forces of supply and demand determine prices and production decisions.

Nontariff Barriers. Government restrictions or barriers to trade other than tariff barriers. These barriers include quotas and a variety of non-science-based health and environmental standards. The European Union ban on hormone-treated beef, for example, is a nontariff barrier.

Protectionism. The targeted use of tariffs or nontariff barriers to restrict imports for the benefit of the domestic producers.

Reciprocity. International trade practice under which a nation grants a particular trade concession or benefit to nationals of another state in exchange for the same concession being offered to its nationals by the corresponding state. Reciprocity is often confused with national treatment.

Retaliation. Punitive trade actions by a nation against another nation in response to a pattern or practice that burdens or restricts trade or market access. Retaliation may also be undertaken by a nation when its trading partner raises a tariff outside the framework of the World Trade Organization. Under the WTO dispute settlement mechanism, retaliation may be permitted after other attempts to settle the dispute have failed. Retaliation under the WTO must equal the value of trade lost by the offending practice and may be in sectors other than the sector complained of.

Services. A range of nonmanufacturing economic activities including health care, telecommunications, financial services, education, entertainment, travel, and tourism. The service sector accounts for over 25 percent of global trade. An agreement on services was recently included within the WTO framework.

Subsidy. A financial contribution provided directly or indirectly by a government or any public body that confers a benefit to manufacturers of a particular good. Subsidies distort trade and are considered an unfair trade practice. Examples of direct subsidies are cash grants or export bonuses paid directly to a firm by a government. Subsidies may also be indirect, such as subsidies to infrastructure, energy, or inputs to production.

Tariff. A tax imposed by a nation on goods entering the nation. Tariffs may be based on the value of the good imported (ad valorem) or on the quantity of goods imported. Tariffs distort trade by increasing costs of imported goods. In international trade, however, tariffs are less distortive than quotas or voluntary restraint agreements. Tariffs average 4 percent on most goods traded among WTO members. The United States maintains a harmonized tariff schedule, which lists the applicable tariffs for products entering the country.

Transparency. Doctrine of international trade that encourages regulations and laws to be clearly visible to foreign parties. An example of increased transparency is a provision that government procurement practices require posting of bid requirements and dates for submitting bids. A lack of transparency may be a nontariff barrier.

Unfair Trade Practices. Trade distortive practices such as government subsidies or dumping by individual firms. Unfair trade practices may be countered by the imposition of antidumping duties or countervailing duties. Countries and firms that engage in unfair trade practices do so to increase their competitive positions in global markets.

Valuation. Appraised value by customs officers of goods imported. After valuation, the applicable rate of duty is applied by customs.

Pursuant to the GATT valuations agreement, the principal method of valuation must be the actual transaction value, the price paid for the goods under an arms-length transaction.

Voluntary Restraint Agreements (VRAs). Informal arrangements through which exporters voluntarily restrain certain exports, usually through export quotas, to avoid economic dislocation in an importing country and to avert the possible imposition of mandatory import restrictions.

Index

Copyright Office, 110
Copyrights. *See* Intellectual property
Countervailing duties, 51, 54, 58, 60, 135
    agricultural products, 49–50
    definitions, 48, 57–58
    environmental compliance, 50
    injury analysis, 57–60
    investigations, 49, 56–57
Court of International Trade, 27–28, 56, 124, 133n. A.18
Crawford, Carol, 73, 74
Critical circumstances, 58, 67
Crown Central Petroleum Corporation, 90
Cumulation, 52, 55–57
Customs Court, 133n. A.18
Customs Court Act of 1980, 124
Customs Service, 30, 97, 121

Dam, Kenneth, 12
Declaration of Independence, 8
Democratic Party, 10
Department of Commerce. *See also* Dumping
    as administrative authority on dumping, 26–27, 32, 36–37
    agency in international trade, 119–20
    dumping investigations, 28–29, 30, 31–37, 45–47, 127n. 3.3
    national security investigations, 83–93
    subsidy investigations, 52, 57
Department of Defense, 84, 86–87
Department of Energy, 85, 89
Department of Justice, 84
Department of the Navy, 88
Department of State, 120
Department of the Treasury, 25–26, 121
Direct Investment Fund, 123
Disadvantaged regions, 50, 53
Domestic Injection Molding Machinery Trade Group of the Society of the Plastics Industry, 83
Drawback, 135

Dumping
    anticircumvention measures, 36–37
    antidumping orders, 46–47
    calculations, 26–27, 31–37, 42–43
    changed circumstances petition, 46–47
    Court of International Trade, 124
    defense against, 27
    definitions, 11, 23, 38–39, 135
    effects of, 23–24, 30, 41–45
    General Agreement on Tariffs and Trade, 14–15, 26
    injury investigations and determinations, 37–45
    investigations, 28–45
    legislation, 25–28, 35, 36–37, 38–39, 41–42, 43–44, 45
    margins, 26–27, 31–32, 36, 45–46
    market values, 28, 31
    pricing issues, 23–24, 25–26
    reverse dumping, 23
    social dumping, 21
    suspension and revocation of investigations, 30, 45–47
    withdrawal of petitions, 46
Dunlap, Charles, 90

EC. *See* European Community
Eckes, Alfred, 80–81
Economic issues. *See also* Dumping
    competition, 4, 21, 23–24, 26, 62
    domestic industries and, 96
    employment and unemployment, 72–73, 85
    international economy, 3
    Trade Act of 1930, 12
    trade in open markets, 21
Embargo, 135
Engineering Multiplier Program, 123
Environmental issues, 50, 90
Erythropoietin, 95
Escape clause. *See* Section 201
European Community (EC), 107, 108, 117

About the Author

WILLIAM H. LASH III is on the faculty of George Mason University School of Law; he teaches international trade, international business transactions, corporate law, and securities regulation. He is Distinguished Senior Fellow at the Center for the Study of American Business at Washington University.

Mr. Lash had been an attorney with Fried, Frank, Harris, Shriver & Jacobson. He was appointed counsel to the chairman of the U.S. International Trade Commission in 1988.

He received his B.A. from Yale University and his J.D. from Harvard Law School.

This book was edited by
Ann Petty of the publications staff
of the American Enterprise Institute.
The index was prepared by Julia Petrakis.
The text was set in Palatino,
a typeface designed by
the twentieth-century Swiss designer
Herman Zapf.
Cynthia Stock, of Silver Spring,
Maryland, set the type,
and Edwards Brothers, Incorporated,
of Lillington, North Carolina,
printed and bound the book,
using permanent acid-free paper.

The AEI Press is the publisher for the American Enterprise Institute for Public Policy Research, 1150 Seventeenth Street, N.W., Washington, D.C. 20036; *Christopher DeMuth,* publisher; *Ann Petty,* editor; *Leigh Tripoli,* editor; *Cheryl Weissman,* editor; *Alice Anne English,* production manager.